Writing Out Loud

by Deborah Morgan

Grass Roots Press

Writing Out Loud

Cover artwork by Barb Hartmann
Book design and layout by Terry McGuire
Printed by Quality Color Press Inc.

Additional copies of *Writing Out Loud*
can be obtained from the publisher:

Grass Roots Press
A division of Literacy Services of Canada Ltd.
PO Box 52192, Edmonton, Alberta T6G 2T5, Canada
Phone: (780) 413-6491
Fax: (780) 413-6582
Email: grassrt@telusplanet.net
Web: www.literacyservices.com

National Library of Canada Cataloguing in Publication Data

Morgan, Deborah, 1954-
Writing Out Loud

2nd ed.
ISBN 1-894593-16-2

1. English language – Composition and exercises – Study and teaching. 2. Adult education. I. Title

PN148.M67 2002 808'-042'0715 C2001-903557-8

Printed in Canada

Dedicated to all the students throughout Alberta
who had the courage to try writing out loud

Especially
Alice Kneeland
Barb MacTavish
Sharron Szott
Carol Tabone

Table of Contents

Introduction to Second Edition

So much has happened since *Writing Out Loud* came out in 1997. None of us ever dreamed so many people would be interested in the work we did in the Chapters Program or that so many wonderful opportunities would come our way because of it.

Originally referred to as the "*Chapters Handbook*", the first copies of *Writing Out Loud* were made available to the members of the Literacy Coordinators of Alberta through Chapters Project funding. Their response to our practical and innovative ideas to encourage writing was overwhelmingly positive. I put a map of Alberta on my office wall to show the students of Chapters (who had contributed so much of themselves to *Writing Out Loud*) all the places the book had traveled to. We marked each location with a yellow-headed pin.

Through word of mouth, *Writing Out Loud* caught many people's attention. Even though the Chapters Program had come to an end, the number of yellow dots continued to grow and it wasn't long before the map of Alberta gave way to a full map of Canada. Orders for *Writing Out Loud* came in from places the students had never heard of – Rankin Inlet, Sioux Lookout, and Antigonish. The first printing lead to a second and then a third. Without knowing it, we had created a resource that addressed an area of literacy that people obviously wanted to learn more about.

Through the demand for *Writing Out Loud*, we also discovered that a surprising number of literacy workers were not comfortable teaching writing. Even though they understood the importance of writing, they lacked confidence in their own ability to write and had difficulty inspiring students to put words on paper. Based on these findings, we developed the Write to Learn Project to raise awareness of the benefits of writing and to offer training and encouragement to those wishing to include more writing in their literacy work. Through generous funding from the National Literacy Secretariat, we were able to do more groundbreaking work to encourage students and instructors to write and learn together and experience writing as a means of both personal and academic development. Over the past three years, we have researched how writing was being used and valued in literacy programming, traveled across Canada presenting what the students called "Fearless Writing" workshops, and trained literacy workers in all regions of the country to become *Writing Out Loud* Instructors. We had a wonderful time working on this project. We are more convinced than ever that writing is important and are excited to see the growing appreciation for writing development within the literacy community.

Now, the new map of the World on my wall acts as a reference for the copies of *Writing Out Loud* that have found their way to the United States, England and Australia. What started out as an attachment to a government final report for the Chapters Program, has become an internationally acclaimed resource. And now, thanks to Grass Roots Press, what started as a binder full of printed pages we assembled ourselves has become this newly edited, beautifully redesigned book.

And that's not all! Through the willingness of the people who took part in the Write to Learn Training Project to share their ideas and experiences, we will soon have a new resource to promote writing. *More Writing Out Loud* includes writing exercises from literacy programs across Canada and takes a more in-depth look at the challenges and rewards of teaching writing.

When I told the women from Chapters there was going to be another volume of *Writing Out Loud*, they were very excited. One of the women laughed and said, "Hey, maybe *Writing Out Loud* will be like the Chicken Soup books!"

"With all that's happened since *Writing Out Loud* came out five years ago," I said, "anything is possible!"

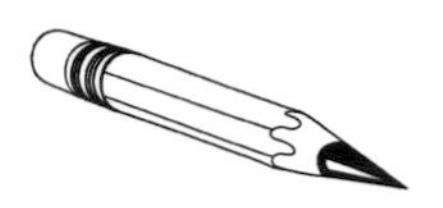

I would like to extend my warmest thanks to Pat Campbell and Grass Roots Press for bringing new life and a new look to this book; Pat Fahy for years of unfailing support; Yvette Souque and Keith Anderson for continuing to value this work; Jerome Martin and his family for taking Writing Out Loud to new heights; Jake the Snake for being able to make visions into reality; Barb Hartmann for giving new meaning to "writing instruments"; and Judith Tomlinson for helping to polish these pages.

Deborah Morgan
January, 2002

Getting Ready

Literacy workers know that the ability to read is extremely important to living fully and productively in today's society. But what about the ability to write? We tend to forget that everything we read had to have been written by someone first.

An amazing number of people don't like to write. Not just literacy students, but teachers, labourers, and business people too. I have heard people say over and over again that they're not any good at writing, or that they have nothing interesting to say. I disagree! People have wonderful stories to tell and most people, when given a little encouragement, discover they are much better writers than they thought they were.

Putting words on paper isn't something we should shy away from. There are significant benefits to be gained through writing. Trying out some of the exercises in *Writing Out Loud* will show you that writing can actually help people begin to:

- look at their lives in a more positive way.
- explore ideas they feel uncomfortable talking about.
- connect their thoughts and feelings.
- identify their values and hopes and goals.
- validate their stories and their lives.
- improve their literacy skills (writing, reading and thinking).
- solve personal conflicts and problems.
- see that they can effectively express and communicate ideas.
- move forward in their lives.

Pretty powerful stuff. Are you wondering how students just beginning to learn to write can experience all these benefits? Keep reading. Writing is not an activity for famous authors only; writing is something we can all enjoy – you and me and those of us with very basic skills. If you are already an avid writer, I hope you will pass your enthusiasm on to others. If writing is still something that makes you uncomfortable, keep reading. You'll be looking around for a pen and some paper in no time.

I encourage you and your student(s) to do more writing together. Learn what it means to write out loud. Dive in and feel all the feelings the words in your head and heart can express. Write together, learn together. Stand up, read your words out loud, feel them, enjoy them, write them in capital letters. Let go, have fun, write, and then write some more.

Handbook Design and Use

Using the Handbook

This handbook is designed to take you on a bit of a journey. The beginning of the book is a starting point, but the journey doesn't have to go in one direction. *Writing Out Loud* is also designed to encourage you to play with ideas and exercises at your own pace, in your own way. The exercises can be adapted, changed, built on, or skipped altogether.

Getting Ready talks about where the idea for this handbook came from and what you need to know to use the exercises in the handbook.

Starting Out is a series of writing exercises that will help you and your student(s) start writing together.

Having Fun provides some exercises to help put some fun into your writing.

Taking Risks introduces writing exercises that will help you stretch your thinking as you become more comfortable with writing.

Building Confidence has more advanced writing exercises and information about polishing and publishing your work.

Feeling Good is full of quotes and information from students and instructors who have tried these exercises and discovered the value of writing.

The Bibliography is an extensive list of books that are helpful resources in areas of writing, learning, creativity and personal development. It is an annotated bibliography including book reviews done by students.

When you spend some time with *Writing Out Loud*, you will understand what I mean when I say that it is designed to take you on a journey. For any journey we embark on, we plan and get ready, start out on the trip, discover there are some risks we have to take a long the way, have some fun and build a lot of confidence through the process. Then we sit down, look back and feel good about all that we learned and all the things we went through.

Learning never ends, nor does this journey. But for many of us, our learning takes us all over the place – into valleys and to the tops of mountains. Tthe going is sometimes tough, sometimes easy. We just need to remember that it's not the destination that is important, it's the journey.

Using the Exercises

The exercises are designed to provide you with clearly laid-out instructions and ideas for encouraging writing.

Title: Each writing exercise has a title followed by an introductory description of where the idea for the exercise came from and/or how the exercise was developed.

Exercise Steps: Detailed steps are given to "walk you through" the exercise so that you will know exactly what to do to get results from the exercise.

Writing Examples: Each exercise is enhanced with samples of student writing related to the theme of the exercise. Some samples are taken from past Chapters publications and some are "first drafts".

Adaptations: In this section I have tried to give you additional information about using the exercise with different literacy levels, classroom settings and one-to-one tutoring. I have also included some ideas for processing the written responses.

Reflections: Under this heading I talk about how each exercise affected me as an instructor – what I learned and what I might do differently next time.

Nine literacy and life skills instructors field tested this handbook so that it would be as user-friendly as possible. The design is a result of their experience in using *Writing Out Loud.*

(Message posted on The Chapters Café, October 1996)

Bravo! We have been having a lot of fun trying out some of the ideas in Writing Out Loud. *I am using the exercises with a group of eight ESL students. One tutor has started using the handbook (two more are still thinking about it). I just gave the tutor the handbook without any coaching, just asked her to look it over and decide if she wanted to give some of the ideas a try... The tutor's first comments were that the manual was very easy to read, clearly laid out, had some really neat ideas and she especially liked having the examples included.*

Veronica Park
Literacy Coordinator, Wetaskiwin

A little bit of history...

Writing Out Loud is about writing. But it's also about a learning readiness program in Camrose, Alberta, called Chapters[1] – a program that changed many people's thoughts and ideas about the value of writing and the value of life. Before we get to the writing exercises, it is important to provide you with a bit of a history of the Chapters Program.

The first year of the Chapters Program (1994/95)

I was introduced to some people on Social Assistance who were really discouraged with where they were in their lives. They wanted (and needed) to find work, but they didn't know how to go about it. They didn't want to go back to school because of past failures. They were tired of being forced to go to employment programs or job placements that they were not able, for a variety of personal reasons, to fully commit to. They wanted to be off Assistance, but they didn't know where to begin to find a way that would work for them. They wanted to design something that would work.

We spent many, many hours around my kitchen table working on a proposal that combined the ideas of "preparing for life" and getting ready for employment. Literacy was also a part of the proposal, because the group was genuinely keen to learn. They wanted to feel good about their learning but they didn't know how to make that happen. They wanted to call the program "Chapters" because they were looking forward to starting a new chapter in their lives. It was eight months before anyone would take us seriously enough to fund the project. By that time, the original group of people who had helped write the proposal had moved on.

My journal entry for February 17, 1994

The first day of Chapters - exhilarating and exhausting all at once.

It seems that some of the students know each other (although I'm not sure all their past connections are positive ones). Other than our interviews, their faces were as new to me as I'm sure mine was to them. Everyone was pretty cautious and quiet sitting around the table, except Cindy.

Cindy - black boots and a black leather jacket, bright red hair and a smoky voice. "You know Deborah", she said after I had done an introduction of the program. "You sure asked me some pretty

[1] Please note that the Chapters Program is not affiliated with the Chapters Bookstores.

personal questions when you interviewed me last week. Did you ask everyone those questions?" I explained that I had, and then looking defiantly around the room, Cindy threw out a challenge. "So who gets to ask YOU those questions?"

Fair enough, I thought. I found a copy of the interview questions and gave it to Cindy. She started off by asking me about my family and how many kids I have. When she was satisfied with my answers, she passed the sheet to the student next to her. Everyone took a turn asking me questions – from my experience in school to what medication I'm on to how I feel about sharing my stories with others.

I was surprised by how hard I found some of the questions. I wasn't very comfortable talking about the alcoholism in my family or how I cope with having MS and why I dropped out of University. But the students seemed to really appreciate my honesty, and I sure had a better understanding of what they went through being interviewed by me. We talked a lot about authority and why they don't like being "told" what to do or how to do it. They want to learn, but they don't want me to teach "at" them and they don't want me to assume I know what's best for them. I really liked what they said to me today. I think we're on fairly equal ground with each other right now and it feels right.

Simply put, the students in the Chapters Program wanted and needed to be treated like whole human beings – people with real lives and real stories. This was not something they were used to. Years of poverty and getting bumped around in the welfare system had left them feeling bruised and afraid. I learned very quickly that the needs of the students were much greater than I had originally anticipated. They were people referred to by the social worker as "high needs clients". My background was in literacy; I thought he meant that they had low literacy skills and high learning needs. But it was much more complicated than that. Many had come from extremely abusive situations, some had serious emotional problems (and diagnosed illnesses such as multiple personality disorder and schizophrenia), some were dealing with alcohol and drug addictions and almost all were on high doses of antidepressants and tranquillizers. I remember the group who helped me write the proposal talking about wanting to be part of "the real world" or having a "real life". I was only just beginning to understand.

As I became more aware of the problems, I also realized that we wouldn't get anywhere if all we did was dwell on problems. I really wanted to get to know the students as individuals, to know what was important to them now and what their hopes were for the future. The first thing that became really clear was their need to feel safe. They needed to know that I wasn't going to hurt them and that this program was not intended to set them up for another failure.

The first thing we did was make the classroom a safe, comfortable place to be. This became even more important when I heard how many of the students felt uncomfortable in their own homes (low income basement rental suites with few windows, unsupportive partners, young children with behavioural problems, lack of food and clothing). We bought second-hand furniture and made one end of the classroom into a "living room" area. We found a radio, a coffeemaker and a microwave at a garage sale and the students brought plants, afghans, pictures and coffee mugs from home. What was once a large, empty room with four bare walls became a space we all felt really good about.

We decided to have the program run from 9:30 a.m. to 3:00 p.m. to respect the needs of the moms in the group. We made decisions about the program together. We were designing a program around trust, hope and a sense of community, and we felt really good about that, too.

My journal entry for May 23, 1994

It's been almost 3 months since the Chapters classroom started. The one male student we had has moved back to Ontario, so we are a woman's group now which feels really comfortable. The magic and the chemistry of our first week together is still happening. I keep wanting to explain to my colleagues what I mean by "magic", but I don't have the words yet. They roll their eyes at me when I talk about Chapters but I really don't care. I know, without any doubt, that there is exceptional learning going on here, for all of us.

I'm not using a curriculum. Everyday real life provides all the ideas I need. I'm not teaching the literacy and employability skills I had in my planning notes; it's so obvious that the students need to find some balance and stability in their lives first. As I teach them what they want to know, they are teaching me what I need to learn, and somehow in that process, we are growing stronger together.

We talk a lot about strengths instead of weaknesses, capabilities instead of disabilities. We take one step at a time - celebrating each small step, each small success. We applaud and cry and laugh in the process. We allow ourselves to be real, to fall down and get up again. We help each other. Each of the students is different, with different needs, but they are all trying to move forward, using whatever strengths they can muster. I really admire that.

Sometimes I think Chapters is like a "walk-in clinic"- a place where people come to heal their broken spirits and, more importantly, their broken learning. Somewhere along the way, their belief in their ability to learn got badly damaged. Their trust in their ability to think just shut down. It's hard to have a spirit, a sense of self, when you don't believe that you're capable or even worthy of learning.

We always talk about self-esteem in our literacy circles, but what is self-esteem? Our belief in ourselves, our inherent knowledge that we are capable human beings? I think it's much more than that. Feeling "capable" has to include our ability to learn, our desire to learn - to try, take risks, touch, enjoy, experiment with life and living. When we believe that we are capable learners, then it seems that anything is possible. Then we can participate in life and contribute to life and feel good about who we are. As each of the women in Chapters grasps this idea, something wonderful happens. Magic? I don't know. I just know that I don't want to be any where in the world but here - here in the Chapters classroom.

By the end of the first year I had convinced the funders of the program that we needed to slow down and rethink the program goals. We needed to allow people the time to become personally ready before they could "get out there and get a job". And I wanted time to study and work with the concepts of personal and learning readiness.

By the end of the first year, we were also doing a great deal of writing. We used writing as a way to tell our stories, and clarify what was important to us and where we wanted to go from here. (I always say "we", because the students weren't the only ones who were learning and growing.) We wrote and put together three "sold-out" publications in eight months. I think my favourite was one called “Rediscover Learning, Rediscover Life”. This publication was a celebration of what learning meant to the women in Chapters. They were like little kids discovering toys in a sandbox. Look what I found! Look what I know! Look what I can do! Their joy and enthusiasm were wonderfully infectious. And finally, people in the field were starting to notice that something special was happening at Chapters.

> *“I think practitioners will welcome the Chapters experience and suggestions because they know they lack ways of identifying student’s very basic needs, and of allowing adult students to remain adults while they are seeking help and trying to change their lives. Chapters keeps the students central and responsible for their own programs and actions. This is far better than trying to ‘fix’ students, or dwelling on their ‘dysfunctions’. Chapters promotes focus on personal growth and personal problem-solving, within the context of learning. Often in other programs, the focus is shifted to therapy and away from learning. If someone needs therapy they should get it; if they need time to reflect, relate, experiment, learn, get encouragement, and plan change, they should be in Chapters.”*
>
> *Dr. Pat Fahy*
> *Athabasca University*

Chapter 2 (1995/96)

We called the second year of funding for the Chapters Program, Chapter 2. As an instructor/facilitator, I could see that I was teaching personal development as much or more than I was teaching literacy. I was working in areas of self-esteem, conflict resolution, life management and goal setting. I could see that literacy and life skills went hand in hand, but it was really only a guess on my part; I knew nothing about the philosophy and methodology of life skills.

I had heard about Life Skills Coaches Training offered at Medicine Hat College (and their commitment to providing life skills instruction to students) and decided it was time to take the course. The 50 hours of training were fantastic; years of questions and uncertainly about the “human” side of my literacy work were answered. I was relieved to know I was on the right track.

Allen VandenBerg, Manager of Employment and Adult Development Programs for Medicine Hat College (and a life skills coach himself) suggested that Medicine Hat College host the grant for Chapter 2 so that I could tap into their resources to further study the connection between literacy and life skills.

We put a terrific research team together. Glenda Staples, who teaches the Life Skills Coaches Training Course as well as life skills in various training and educational programs for Medicine Hat College; Allen VandenBerg, who agreed to be the administrative liaison for the project, and Terry McGuire in Camrose, who had been working with me in the Chapters Program from the beginning as the computer consultant and instructor for the students. With our combined expertise in life skills, administration, computer-mediated communication and literacy, and with the real-life experiences and generosity of a terrific group of students (in Camrose and Medicine Hat) we spent a year looking more closely at how student's personal needs are related to their learning needs. And we kept writing.

My journal for entry September 25, 1995

Notes to Allen: I've been reading over old notes and new notes, trying to fill my head with all we've learned and all the possibilities there are for our research with Chapters.

I keep coming back to the idea of learning readiness - people being able to see/view themselves as capable learners. This is the crux of so much. When we believe we can learn, we are able to hope and take risks and look at life with less fear and more enthusiasm. Without the basic belief that we can learn (and that learning is a good thing) we are not able to live life fully.

BUT - there is a necessary stage for people to go through to begin thinking about being able to learn. They have to be awake first, personally ready.

"Being awake" means being able to think and feel. Many people who come to our programs are so numb from the pain in theirs lives, that the ability to think and feel has been turned off. They have needed to do that for survival. They have turned off their senses, to spare their hearts and minds any more feeling. Even when a difficult situation has passed or been resolved, that "numbness" remains as a coping mechanism. This is not necessarily a conscious decision. It is simply survival.

Most students enter into a program because of crises or need. Something has happened to change their thinking:

"Maybe I better go back to school - I can't find a job."

"I'm never going to get anywhere if I don't learn to read better."

"Social Services is going to cut me off if I don't start looking for work.""My kids are going to end up just as dumb as I am."

When these students come to our programs, are they awake, personally ready? I would certainly think some are, the more fortunate ones, but the neediest students (and so many of our students are "high needs") are probably not. We can't begin to teach students and have them listen and understand, until they are mentally and physically able to receive and process information.

So, to back track a little, we have identified our continuum of Readiness.

Personal — Learning — Employment

This continuum idea seems to work; the students can see where they fit on the continuum, where their strengths are and what areas they need to work on. The model has been really well received by many agencies such as Canada Employment Centre and Social Services. We are able to apply it with good understanding to all of the existing programs we have - from Chapters to Basic Job Readiness Training.

We've identified the students and their needs and realities (ie. to move forward in their lives and to make sense out of their lives) and we recognize the goals/needs of the educators and students' support agencies (ie. to teach literacy skills and prepare people for employment). **What I think is so amazing about what's happening here is that the Chapters approach to life and learning says that we can help all involved move towards or reach their identified goals through the use and value of writing.**

Writing is creative and non-intrusive and allows for thought and discussion and growth and self-discovery. In other words, literacy instruction must allow for personal growth so that the *skills learned can be used and valued. Otherwise, they are simply skills learned in isolation from real life. There are those who say that creativity sparks the soul. Writing is extremely creative and we want to spark the souls and spirits of our students. When that happens, they are able to take a much more active and productive role in their own learning.*

Writing became the student's means of discovering and identifying personal and academic needs. And writing became the means that we as researchers and instructors used to better understand the needs of the students. The students and researchers worked together as a team to find ways to teach and learn that were relevant to us. We all agreed that students must be personally ready and comfortable with themselves as learners before they could effectively enter into concentrated academic or employability programs. And we discovered how powerful the use of computers can be in both literacy and life skills training. During Chapter 2 we produced three more sold out publications with the last one involving student writing from students in both Camrose and Medicine Hat.

As researchers, Glenda, Allen, Terry and I put aside our agendas, openly recognizing that the needs and interests of the students had to come first. What the students wanted to learn, how they learned and how they felt about learning became the foundation of our thinking. What we started to call "the Chapters process" recognized each student as a whole, likable and capable person, no matter what their background or history might have been. This positive starting point paved the way for students to get past their fears, become involved in their own learning, and speak about and identify their individual needs and hopes.

We came to understand that for many literacy/life skills students, the "needs" we talk about are not just learning needs, but rather personal needs that have to be dealt with before effective learning can take place. We talked about self-esteem, but also about housing security, child care, protection from violence, emotional and physical stability, and basic nutrition. We understand better now that self-esteem comes as a result of caring about what we call "human being basics". We all need to feel like functioning human beings before we can see ourselves as capable or even interested learners.

We learned that the kind of writing we did in the Chapters Program, writing from the heart, is actually a journey in personal discovery, a gentle way for people to get to know themselves better. Thoughts come forward in simple, honest, heart-felt words – words we can understand – that are in our own language. As instructors, we need to recognize and celebrate these thoughts and ideas as the students' personal curricula. They will learn what they need to learn as they need to learn it. We are simply (but importantly) facilitators and encouragers in that process.

Chapter 3 (1996/97)

The handbook you are now holding is the result of a tremendous team effort to bring our understanding about literacy, life and learning to you in a useful, practical way. *Writing Out Loud* is more than a series of writing exercises. It is a resource about how the learning of the students and instructors who work with these exercises can be processed and valued so that the learning can be real and meaningful to everyone.

We have come a long way from when a group of discouraged but resourceful people met with me around my kitchen table to work on the proposal for Chapters. It makes me feel good to see how close we've come to fulfilling their original dreams. The group wanted to learn and to change, but they wanted to be treated like real people in the process. They were tired of being told what they didn't know and what they needed to (or should) know. They wanted to feel capable; they wanted to have some say in what the next steps in their lives were to be. They wanted to feel a part of a community and they wanted to feel good about what they were doing. I hope someday the people who gave this program its name will be able to benefit from its success.

The Chapters Program has given me the insight to look into myself and find out what I want to do with my life. I see so many friendly faces here that have all had good times and bad times but know all is not lost. By being here we know that there is something out there for all of us. I think if the Chapters Program was not running or never started, we all would be in the same rut as before. Afraid to try new ideas. We would be afraid to go after our goals and dreams. I feel I would lose or never gain any self-esteem which this program has given me.

I'm starting to feel good about myself. I am starting to make changes in my life. Changes for the better. Don't take this away from me.

Sherry
Chapters, Camrose

Questions About Writing and the Writing Process

Teaching writing begins with you, the tutor/instructor. You may find that the exercises in *Writing Out Loud* will challenge you as well as your student. You may find that your own comfort level with writing isn't where you would like it to be. That's okay! One of the benefits of a handbook like this, is that it encourages a team approach to learning. You are probably full of questions. Let me see if I can answer some of them for you.

My student says he doesn't like to write. What can I do to help him feel more comfortable with writing?

The first thing we need to do is establish a sense of "safety". When we feel safe, we are much more willing to try new ideas and have fun with our learning. By "safe", I mean feeling comfortable, at ease, accepted, relaxed, unthreatened. We create safe learning environments by making sure we (the student and teacher) are comfortable with one another, that the learning setting (the kitchen table, the library or the classroom) is warm and welcoming, and that there is a feeling of respect and good will between the student and teacher. Trust is important too, but I have found that working together on exercises such as the ones in this handbook can be what builds trust and an even greater sense of safety. When a student feels safe, a willingness to try will follow.

To help the students feel safe in the Chapters classroom, we created a set of guidelines called "The Chapters Commitment". The students took great care in writing and thinking about these guidelines. They revised them and added to them as they felt it necessary. This simple "code of ethics" was a terrific reference for all of us. As each new student joined the program, she was given these guidelines as a starting point. The students had many questions about what is expected of them. I found they really appreciated knowing from the beginning that their feelings and needs (like the "right to pass") would be taken into consideration.

[unedited] At first I was a little worried about writing my thoughts and feelings out on paper but by the end of the lesson I realized that there was no pressure on me to share my work with the rest of the class so I am a lot more comfortable now.

Viv

Basic Job Readiness Training, Medicine Hat

The Chapters Commitment

While I am a participant in the Chapters Program I will do my best to:

- respect the uniqueness and ability of each person in the Program.
- not pass judgement on others and will be fair and helpful with my comments.
- help to create an accepting place to learn.
- be allowed to "pass" on activities that I do not want to take part in.
- respect the people in the program by not using their names or speaking about them or their writing in discussion about the program outside of the classroom.
- give everybody equal opportunity to speak and to take part in the Chapters Program.
- be a good listener.
- give everyone the right to have their own opinion as I have a right to mine.
- understand that it is okay for me to express my own needs (ie. quiet time, time out, etc.).
- contact the coordinator or a classmate if I am unable to attend class as I understand that my being at Chapters is important to my own success and to the success of the Chapters Program.
- play an active part as a member of the team of creative people who are working together to build and shape the Chapters Program.

Signed: ______________________

Dated: ______________________

Does my student have to be a good writer to do these exercises?

The average grade level of the students in the Chapters Program was Grade 7. BUT that doesn't mean these exercises won't work for students who are not writing at as high a level.

These exercises have been field-tested with beginning ESL students, adult basic education students, students in volunteer literacy programs, elementary school students, instructors and program administrators. Some tutors have found success in acting as scribes to help their students tell their stories. And some instructors have simply adapted the exercises to fit the needs and abilities of the students in their classrooms.

With all the students I have worked with, it wasn't their grade level that held them back from writing; it was their confidence. They were "reluctant writers" because they were afraid they would be criticized. Many were embarrassed about their handwriting. Many thought they had nothing to say. Once the students tried "writing from the heart" and had a chance to feel good about putting words on paper, their reluctance was replaced with excitement. No matter what their skill level, they started to look forward to writing opportunities.

My worst subject in high school was English because of the essay writing we had to do. I remember counting the words to see if I had enough for a 500 word essay. My letter writing over the years was only what was absolutely necessary. Listening to Deborah talk about writing from within was very interesting and I found writing we did today much easier than I have ever experienced before.

Gladys
Basic Job Readiness Training, Medicine Hat

What do you mean by "writing from the heart"?

When we talk about writing, most people think about essays, reports and business letters. That's only one kind of writing. The writing I'm talking about in this handbook is what we call "writing from the heart" – writing about how we feel, in words that are as simple as the words we think and speak.

Many people think they can't write because they can't write "well". They think their writing has to be "correct" and assume that if they are not good at spelling or grammar, then they are not good at writing. It took the students a few weeks to believe me when I told them I didn't care about spelling or grammar or what the words looked like on the page. I just wanted them to write – to write for the pure pleasure of it. I explained to them that if we worry about where to put the comma before we start writing, we'll never write anything. Once the students stopped worrying, they started writing. They wrote about things that were important to them, they wrote in their own words and they were amazed by what they had to say. This is writing from the heart.

How do I grade this kind of writing?

Some of you are working in classroom settings with curriculums and specific goals that have to be met. It is important to give students grades or marks for their work. I am not convinced, however, that writing from the heart is something that should be graded. Evaluated perhaps, but not graded.

Instructors have asked me if writing with little concern for spelling and grammar is encouraging "good writing". The initial writing we do is without regard for spelling or grammar, but it's always possible to go back and "polish" what we've written. I have had students so pleased with a certain piece, that they WANT to go back and correct their spelling or improve the structure of the sentences. They will actually ask me correct their work, red pen and all. This is when the grammar lessons are most effective – well after the student believes that he does in fact have the ability to write.

In the Chapters Program, we have an expression we call the "GBT's" or the "Goose Bump Theory". If you read or hear someone's writing and it gives you goose bumps, then it is good writing. Writing from the heart is what gives us the GBT's. The words mean something; they reach deep down inside you and make you think and feel and smile. This kind of writing is where we all need to start. I always encourage the students to polish the pieces of writing that gave us the GBT's because those are the pieces of writing that have the most meaning for them, that they are most proud of.

Writing from the heart takes a lot of courage and a sense of adventure – strengths that are perhaps more valuable in the long run than the knowledge of good grammar. Students should be credited for that courage and willingness to try.

Writing essays and reports is important, but no more important than writing from the heart. Help your students find things to write about that have meaning to them. Let them write in their own words. Encourage them to write and keep writing. The students' writing will improve just from the sheer volume of the words and sentences they put on paper.

> *Perhaps one of the most exciting aspects of the Chapters process is the foundation of being student centred... All of the aspects of the process revolve around students. The topics, learning, resources and activities involve students thoroughly.*
>
> *It is the "interests" of the students which are addressed. It is the resources of the students which are utilized. It is access to additional resources "by" the*

students which form the learning environment. And it is the accomplishments of the students which are identified and celebrated.For some practitioners a shift in traditional thinking must occur. Focusing on curriculum or a series of exercises must be adapted. Instead of setting the framework for learning it is the students' writing which sets the framework in which curriculum "resources" may be most appropriately used. Initial reactions by some practitioners are that this will take more time and fewer "tasks" (curriculum task) must be completed. The realization that students are gaining "specific" skills, of interest to them, means that these skills will directly impact their daily lives. The transference from classroom learning to life is now part of the process.

Allen VandenBerg
Chapters Administrator, Medicine Hat College

How do I encourage reading at the same time that my students are concentrating on writing?

All of the instructions for the writing exercises in *Writing Out Loud* will suggest that everyone read their writing out loud to one another. This may not be comfortable for your student(s), at least not in the beginning. If you read your writing out loud, your students will be encouraged to follow suit. The words that they write make wonderful reading material. The words are familiar (at least by sound) and the content of the writing is of interest and meaning to them. Without realizing it, the students in the Chapters Program were improving both their reading and writing skills, just by writing down their stories and reading them out loud.

I also found that students sometimes wrote about things that reminded me of a book I had read. I would then recommend the book, which they were usually able to find at the local library. When one of the students wrote about her "hot flashes", we found all kinds of written material (books and pamphlets) on menopause to read together. The students also brought in magazine articles they found relating to subjects we had talked about.

I read stories out loud to the students, just so they could hear different authors say things in different ways. They loved being read to and would bring in stories of their own to have me read.

The focus of this handbook is writing, but writing in conjunction with reading certainly makes the writing experience that much richer.

What do I do if my student writes about difficult things that I really don't want to hear about?

All literacy workers have felt "in over their heads" at different times. It is an unavoidable reality that many of our students have very difficult lives and need more support than we as instructors are able to give them. The students entering our programs today have higher needs than ever before.

> *In Alberta there is little debate amongst adult educators that the student population entering the learning environment has changed greatly in the past 5 years. Students are coming in with not only literacy challenges, but also with a whole range of personal issues.*
>
> *The backgrounds are diverse and often devastating. The challenge for the literacy practitioner has become trying to enhance literacy skills while recognizing the personal management issues. It is very difficult for a student to learn while in the midst of crisis.*
>
> *Glenda Staples*
> *Life Skills Coach Trainer, Medicine Hat College*
> *Chapter 2 Final Report*

There have certainly been times that students in the Chapters Program read personal stories that were heart-wrenching, that had us all in tears. What always followed, however, was tremendous support from the other students and a lightness of heart for the student who had read her writing out loud.

I have also found that writing from the heart helps students do some of their own healing work. It helps them identify where there are blocks to moving forward in their lives, what choices they made in the past that perhaps weren't healthy, and more importantly, where their strengths are. In a safe learning environment, they can explore their own feelings and ideas at their own pace.

When we write, we rarely take our writing to a depth that we personally can't handle. If a student is writing about something that happened to her when she was a child, she will write only about what she is able to think about safely. I have seen people in verbal therapy sessions blurt out things that they were obviously not ready to deal with. I have never seen that happen with writing. There is something in the timing of the thought process of getting words on paper that allows for more careful and controlled thought.

Having said that, I also want to assure you that you are not expected to be a counsellor or a therapist. There are support services available in your community that you can refer your students to for extra support or counselling. I have referred students from Chapters to Alberta Mental Health, the Woman's Shelter, the Career Centre, AADAC (Alberta Alcohol and Drug Abuse Commission), AA, and Al-Anon. I work closely with a social worker at Alberta

Social Services to make sure that I know the (ever-changing) rules and guidelines of the Social Assistance system and I make sure that all the students know the local Crisis Hotline number.

I used to panic when my students wrote about difficult things. I'd think, "What should I do? What should I say?" One day, when one of the students wrote about the horrible abuse she had suffered as a child, I blurted out in tears, "I wish I knew what to do to help you". Shelly smiled at me and said: "It's OK Deborah. I didn't expect you to do anything. I just needed someone to listen."

We all need to have our lives and our stories validated. We need to be validated as people. Don't be afraid of writing from the heart because your student might write about difficult things. Getting feelings out is a good thing. Talk to each other, listen to your student, help your student find the resources he needs to help him deal with the issues that might be getting in the way of his learning.

What you're talking about sounds a lot like life skills. Is there a connection between literacy and life skills?

Absolutely! Learning doesn't happen in isolation from real life. I have found that when we openly recognize that real life is actually *part* of learning, the students' learning is much more effective.

> *Chapters helps students to look at their lives, make decisions about that and to set goals. This is largely accomplished through writing. By implementing Chapters "real-life literacy", students are able to develop literacy and life skills simultaneously thus avoiding having to decide which is more important – literacy or life skills.*
>
> *Chapters is able to meet the diverse needs of the students and they enjoy it. This means they attend classes not through threats or pressure, but because they really want to be there. They not only learn to learn, but learn to like learning.*
>
> *Glenda Staples, Life Skills Coach Trainer*
> *Chapter 2 Final Report*

Writing has always been seen as an academic activity. The team of people who worked on this project know now that writing can also be used as a means of self discovery and personal growth. That's the life skills and literacy connection that we are convinced is of great importance to literacy programming today. When we are learning we are growing. When we don't feel capable of learning and don't see learning as a good thing, we are also denying ourselves important opportunities for personal development.

A definition of literacy/life skills currently being used at Medicine Hat College is: *gaining confidence to know I can learn, knowing I am worthy and knowing I have some thing(s) valuable to contribute.*

It can be argued that if teaching literacy skills includes helping students "learn to learn", then teaching literacy skills also means facilitating personal development. We believe that literacy *is* a life skill!

> *I think everyday now is a learning experience to me whether it be good or bad. It's still learning. Learning makes me realize things. I surprise myself lately because I want to learn so much and I'm not afraid anymore to make a mistake. I know I won't crumble if I do. Only one year ago, I remember learning how to fill out withdrawal and deposit slips at the bank. I felt very scared and would be sweating in line thinking I did it wrong. I almost started crying whenever I had to fill out a form of some kind. Now I just do the best I can and I know if I make a mistake it can be fixed. I am really ready to learn now. I think I have let go of the idea that I am stupid and won't learn, so now that I don't have that block in my brain, I have room in there to take in new information and understand it. Now I like learning and will continue to learn for the rest of my life.*
>
> *Carol,*
> *excerpted from* Rediscover Learning, Rediscover Life

Okay, you've convinced me to try more writing with my student. How do I get started?

Keep reading. Spend a little time familiarizing yourself with the exercises in this handbook. Imagine trying some of the ideas with your student. The next time you get together with your student, tell him you want to to try something a little different. Then just go for it; as you both learn and grow, you'll find your literacy work more enjoyable than ever.

Starting Out

Many people think they aren't writers because they haven't written a novel or been published. While few of us will ever write a book, the things we write about are still valuable and important. A writer is simply someone who writes – a lot. *Writing Out Loud* will give you plenty of ideas to write about so that you will be able to encourage more people to see themselves as capable writers. And hopefully, more people will discover the true pleasure of writing in the process.

This section of *Writing Out Loud* offers simple exercises to help you and your student(s) get started writing together. The "writing together" part of this handbook is really important. You may be someone who isn't very confident about your own writing – this handbook and these exercises are as much for you as they are for your student(s). You get to write and have fun, too!

You can let your student(s) know that this is new and scary for you too. Then, let yourselves go, encourage one another and you'll be amazed at what comes out on paper.

Freewriting

I start every writing class with five minutes of freewriting. Nothing centers the students as well or encourages free expression more.

What is freewriting? Just as it sounds, it is a time to write freely, without worry about what to write or what will "come out". The whole idea is to keep your pen moving, allowing thoughts to come onto the paper as they will. Freewriting is a little bit like journaling, but it is a timed activity that doesn't have specific goals – except to write as much as possible for the given time period.

Exercise Steps

1. You will need a pen/pencil, a clean sheet of paper (a notebook is fine, too) and a timer. I started off with a portable stove-top timer, but we all decided that it was much too loud and jarring when the bell rang. A watch timer is much quieter. Sometimes I just mark the time at the top of the page and watch for when 5 minutes is up.

   I always encourage my students to date their pages – especially with freewriting. This makes it easy to go back and look at the progress the student has made, both personally and academically.

2. Explain to the student(s) that the idea for this exercise is simply to write – about absolutely anything. If nothing comes to mind, simply write, "I can't think of anything to write" and keep going. Remember – punctuation, spelling and grammar are not important right now. The goal of writing from the heart is just to write.

3. Set the timer and start writing. You too! When five minutes are up, tell the student(s) to finish their sentences, put their pens down and take a deep breath. (Some instructors prefer to have the students put their pens down the second the time is up, but the Chapters students found this too frustrating and asked if they could at least finish their sentences – not their thoughts necessarily, just the sentences.)

4. In the Chapters Program we encouraged one another to read our freewriting out loud. This is voluntary; students always have the option to "pass" if they want to. Sometimes a student will choose not to read her freewriting, but would show it to me later or read it at the end of the class. In most cases, the students looked forward to reading their thoughts out loud and listening to the thoughts of others.

Writing Examples

March 14, 94

[unedited] I just got back to class from lunch. I had a seafood sub at a new restaurant. It was really grose! I went with John and Tina. There lunch looked better than mine. I think tomorrow I will bring my own lunch and just stay here and eat it. I think that would be better than wasting $5.00 on something that's disgusting! It's now freewriting I don't no what else to write about. Deborah says we have 5 minutes for this I hope the time is running out because I have nothing else to say except so far my day has gone well. The computer was fun and it was alot easier than I thought it would be. Now I can finaly say I have used a computer.

March 16, 94

[unedited] I just finished my lunch again. John brought it to me it was nice to see his handsom face. I will miss him alot and I have such mixed feeling about him leaving. I don't no what is wrong with me. Why don't i ever no what I want. I wish I could slide into sombody elses body for a day so I can feel what it is like to feel your feelings normilly because I no its being abused all my life that I get my feelings so mixed up its so hard! I am so glad that my kids can express there feelings so well that is really healthy. I wish I new how it worked but I just don't! I wonder if in time it will naturally come.

Carol
Chapters, Camrose

(Note: When Carol first started freewriting, she would concentrate so hard and push so hard with her pen that her page would actually curl! She later found that writing with a pencil suited her better. She especially liked the "scritching" sound of the pencil moving on the paper.)

Dec. 6, 96

[unedited] Today is going to be an awesome day because we haven't done hardly anything all day we've played on the computers and now we are free writing then going to have a test then we're out of here and the I can go and get just wrecked after school and after my ADDAC thing with my mom which will be great fun. I can't think of anything to say right now cause my hand is starting to hurt and that all I'm thinking about. Last night was fun I went to have tons of fun with my friends we went to Jamie house and played poker with his dad and smoked cigars.

M.K.

Fifth on Fifth Youth Services, Lethbridge

Adaptations

Instructors always ask me why we do freewriting for five minutes. Well, we tried three minutes but that didn't seem to be enough time to "get going" and seven minutes was just too exhausting! Five minutes seems to work the best.

I haven't tried freewriting with less experienced writers. Five minutes would probably be too much, and yet I have had students at a Grade 2-3 level who were pleased with writing one or two sentences. Even one-word thoughts would be a good start.

Reflections

It is through listening to my students' freewriting that I was able to get a sense of how they were feeling, what was important to them, and what was on their minds.

On a lovely spring afternoon in April (when I was feeling particularly cheerful), I learned as the students read their thoughts out loud, that someone most of them knew had died of AIDS the night before. I put aside my "joys of spring" lesson plan; we spent the afternoon talking about death, illness, funerals and making wills instead. For the students, freewriting allows them an opportunity to let go of the everyday ups and downs they're dealing with outside of the classroom. As an instructor, I could actually see the students begin to relax and settle down to this time of learning.

Some of the students balked at the idea of freewriting at first ("I don't have anything interesting to say", or "There's so much on my mind I don't know where to begin.") but later, if I forgot to do our freewriting, the students right away reminded me. They looked forward to this time of "letting go" and often did freewriting at home (not necessarily timed) to clear their minds when they were going to begin something new or difficult.

On top of all the benefits freewriting provides for new writers and their instructors, it is also a lot of fun! Sometimes there were tears, but more often there was laughter in the classroom when we read our freewriting out loud.

Deborah's Freewriting, September 14, 1994

Its Josh's birthday today. I have been thinking where I was ten years ago today. I was in full labour, not taking it very well. Not coping with the pain very well, scared about the health of the baby, wanting it all to be over. I couldn't bear the idea of losing this baby like I'd lost the twin. I wanted the labour to be over, partly because of the discomfort (big time) but mostly because I wanted to hold the baby and make sure it was breathing.

Josh was born after 16 hours of labour. He was healthy, ten pounds, strong and perfect. I was worried at first because he never cried. When the doctor handed him to me, I noticed that the tape we had brought with us was playing "Send In the Clowns". Ten years later, he is still my little clown.

Word Guides

Most students like freewriting once they get the hang of it, but there are times when someone will say, "I really need some ideas today; my brain just feels dead." This is a good time to use "guided freewriting" where the students write freely around a given word or idea.

Exercise Steps

1. Prepare the student(s) for freewriting (ie. paper, pen and timing device).
2. Give the students(s) a word and ask them to write about it – being as free, imaginative and honest as possible.
3. There are a number of ways to choose a word or idea:

   - Keep a jar or basket full of pieces of paper with one word ideas written on them. The student(s) can pick a word from the jar for a quick writing exercise. If you come across an interesting word or idea in your work together, add that to the jar (words like – learning, angel, mothering, home, trampoline, diaper, report card, interview).
   - Have a student close her eyes, open a dictionary, put her finger on the page then read out loud the word her finger falls on. Write down the word. Be sure the student understands the word's meaning and usage, then write about that word for five minutes.
   - Word lists from magazines such as *Reader's Digest* or from "word-a-day" calendars are also a good source of ideas. Have the student(s) take turns bringing in or finding a word to use for guided freewriting.

4. Read your word interpretations out loud and enjoy the different ways each of you will approach given words or ideas.

Writing Examples

The Chapters students were having a BBQ in the park when we did this writing exercise. I had written some "summertime" words on cards and the students picked these two.

"Shorts"

[unedited] Dirty shorts, clean shorts, any kind, make or length of shorts, I love them. There made to cover only the necessary parts leaving the rest of your body free, easier to move, run, jump, bend, roll over or climb or hike. There's less material which makes for a smaller wash load and less to iron or care for. Jean shorts are my favourite as I can match any top I have with them. I don't like a tight waste in my shorts as I like to be free.

Sharron
Chapters, Camrose

[unedited] Boxers or briefs? Summer shorts, bare legs, sunburned knees. Blue jean shorts with frilled edges. Shorts for men. Too tight shorts - no kids! (heard that today on Dr. Dean Edell) Gym shorts, smelly, sweaty. White shorts for hot days. Shorts to the knees, shorts that show just a bit of cheek. Shorts for some, not for others. Shorts too tight in my bottom drawer. Shorts that show white legs. Shorts, shorts, shorts!

Alice
Chapters, Camrose

"Park"

[unedited] Park. The first thing I think of is parking my car. I really don't like that. I make sure I have a couple of spots so that I get it right. I would rather walk 3 blocks to wear I am going than park in a tight spot. I remember when I was younge someone would say they parked if they went on a date. It meant - well, I think we all no what it meant! I enjoy going to the park. When I took the kids to all the different parks the other day, I told them we were going park hopping. That was a nice night but I forgot the Off.

Carol
Chapters, Camrose

[unedited] I like parks because when you say parks you think of recreation and fun. A good place to have a picnic and hotdogs and Sharron's brownies and even a good place to do writing about parks. Park reminds me of old times with friends and my dogs Tug and Annie. It's a place to enjoy the sun. If you have any, bring your kids and let them run free. It's a break for you and fun for them. Parks are freedom!

Josh
Deborah's son, age 11

Adaptations

Some students find guided free writing more difficult because they have to focus and be more specific in their writing, but others seem to like the structure. I don't often use guided freewriting at the beginning of a writing class, as it takes away from the opportunity for each student to deal with their own immediate thoughts. I do like to use it, however, to get a group working and thinking together (as in the writing samples above).

If you find your student(s) having trouble with freewriting, try a more structured approach for a while, or alternate between freewriting and guided freewriting to see what your student(s) like or respond to best.

Practice at guided freewriting can really help students to look at ideas from all different angles. For new or reluctant writers, it might help to put the word on a blackboard and brainstorm around the word to generate ideas before beginning writing.

If you are teaching a particular topic to your student(s), you could try guided freewriting to begin the unit. Without brainstorming, give the students a word like "communication" or "choices" to write about. (This can also be done for homework for a more advanced group.) After you have shared your writing with one another, discuss the idea, then explain to the students what they will be studying or exploring together.

Reflections

I was always amazed by the imaginations my students had. I could look at or think about a word or an idea one way, then discover through this kind of writing that I had only scratched the surface. Freewriting or this kind of structured writing is very freeing for the mind and soul. The students were always exhilarated after quick exercises like this; they became excited by the thoughts and ideas that would spring forth.

There were always good days and not-so-good days, where one student would get stumped and another would surprise herself with her own written thoughts, but I almost always found this exercise to be entertaining and definitely eye opening.

Success
by Sherry

My idea of success would be to have the frame of mind to accomplish anything I put my mind to. To have the freedom of voice to speak out against injustice. To have the freedom of choice in where my life will lead me. The freedom of value, where I am valued for my ideas, my career choices and for being me. My idea of success would be to have the money to do things I want to do and the choice to do what I want to do without interference from others.

(*excerpted from* New Chapters)

Gratitude Journal

Journaling has always been considered an important form of writing. As an avid journaller myself, I agree. I have encouraged different groups I've worked with to keep regular journals with varying degrees of success.

I recently came across a wonderful book by Sarah Ban Breathnach called *Simple Abundance* which describes the benefits of keeping a Gratitude Journal. Ban Breathnach states that a Gratitude Journal can "change the quality of your life beyond belief". And it's very simple.

Exercise Steps

1. If your program can afford it, purchase a journal or notebook with lined pages for each of the students (and perhaps the tutors, too). A simple way to make each journal unique to the individual is to have the student(s) make a collage from magazine cut-outs on the front cover of an inexpensive scribbler. The theme of "things I'm grateful for" can be used in the decorating process – family photos, recipes, favourite sayings, fabric swatches or a child's drawing. We used clear "MacTac" to cover and protect the collages.

2. Ask your student(s) to write down five things they are grateful for each day. This can be done during class time or at home (or both). It is recommended in *Simple Abundance* that you keep your journal by your bedside and write in it each night before going to sleep. The instructor should take part in this activity as well.

3. Encourage your student(s) to keep this daily journal for at least a month. Have a discussion together at the end of the month to see if you are feeling a little more content with life and with what you have.

Writing Examples

Excerpt from *The Hearts of Women*, a Chapters publication:

As women in the Chapters Program, we are grateful for...
...being alive and changing our lives
...thrift shops and garage sales
...having dreams
...M & Ms and chocolate
...mud and little boys
...the assistance we receive from Social Services
...soft kittens and warm mittens
...making it through each hour, each day
...butterflies and freedom
...the peace and quiet of sleeping children
...our five senses
...freedom of speech and being able to express our opinions
...beautiful sunrises and colourful skies
...each other
...green grass and blue skies
...picnics, hot dogs and ants
...opportunities that encourage us to learn and grow
...big "boys" who fly kites
...friends - big, small, winged and four legged
...starfish and sand castles
...being able to be "home alone" once in a while
...computers that say, "I'm trying to think but nothing happens!"
...the little things in life
...Chapters

Adaptations

This exercise seems to suit everyone. A tutor can act as a scribe for a student, or beginning writers can write one-word answers such as, "I am grateful for birds, my children, Diet Coke, sunshine". As students become more confident with their writing, they will begin to write longer descriptions of what they are grateful for. I also found that at first, students wrote about simple, immediate and tangible things. Then they began to write about themselves and their families: "I am grateful that I got out of the mess I was in with my husband because now I don't have to put up with his yelling at me all the time." Then they wrote about their communities and the world around them: "I am grateful for places that believe in peace. I don't want there to be any more wars. I am glad that Canada isn't like other countries that feel so much hatred."

There are many adaptations and uses for journal writing. One approach I tried was to have students keep journals and hand them in to me once a week. I would respond to their writing, asking questions and giving feedback. With a class of students, this can take extra time, but it does give the instructor the opportunity to build trust and get to know the student(s) better.

I have also tried to encourage students to journal on their own (every day, or every couple of days) but I found that those students who were not comfortable writers did not continue to keep journals. It worked well when I asked a particular student who was experiencing difficulties to keep a journal. This gave the student a healthy way to express her feelings and frustrations (without taking up class time) and me an another way to give the student more support.

Reflections

The Gratitude Journal works. I have kept one for a number of months now, and I have been amazed by what it has taught me and by how much more comfortable I feel with my life – just the way it is. I saw the same results with the women in Chapters. Their attitudes were more positive, they were able to find the good in tough situations, and were more aware of what made them happy.

Sometimes things can get pretty dreary in the classroom. The weather is cold and rainy, and someone comes in with the news that they have been cut back by Social Services because one of their children has moved out. The "blues" can set in very quickly, making teaching much more difficult. But with a more positive outlook, we could talk about the events, develop some strategies, and end with some positive thoughts. After a tough discussion, I would often pass a sheet of paper around that said, "I Am Grateful For..." and have each student write one line. Then I read it out loud to show the students that we still have things in our lives that are good. Recognizing the things we were grateful for helped us to stay focused and keep moving forward.

I hope you will try keeping a Gratitude Journal for yourself. Ban Breathnach says,

> *"As the months pass and you fill your journal with blessings, an inner shift in your reality will occur. Soon you will be delighted to discover how content and hopeful you are feeling. As you focus on the abundance rather than on the lack in our life, you will be designing a wonderful new blueprint for the future. This sense of fulfilment is gratitude at work, transforming your dreams into reality."*

Sense-able Writing

"Living life awake" is an expression the Chapters students used when they were feeling good. They were awake to what was around them, aware of the world. One of the things they appreciated when they were more awake, was that they noticed so much more than when they were "asleep" or just coping day to day.

Feeling awake and alive is a healing, healthy way to be. I have found that writing about our senses and sensitivity to the world around us is a powerful way to help us all wake up and see the world with newness.

I have developed a few exercises isolating the five senses (sight, touch, sound, taste, smell) to help students use their senses more. It is easy to forget how important everyday use of our senses is.

This chapter is laid out a little differently as there are suggested exercises for each of the five senses without a separate heading for Adaptations or Writing Examples.

1. Sight - Eyes

Imagine what the world would be like if you couldn't see. We take our sight so much for granted. Helping students to "open their eyes" and see the world around them really helps them to see more, and to appreciate what they do see.

Exercise Ideas

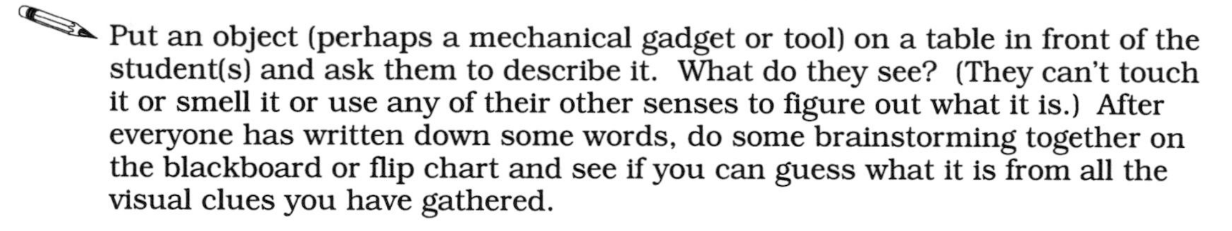

- Put an object (perhaps a mechanical gadget or tool) on a table in front of the student(s) and ask them to describe it. What do they see? (They can't touch it or smell it or use any of their other senses to figure out what it is.) After everyone has written down some words, do some brainstorming together on the blackboard or flip chart and see if you can guess what it is from all the visual clues you have gathered.

- For an assignment, ask your student(s) to go home a different way. Have them describe what they saw that was different from what they usually see.

- If your student(s) have children, ask them to describe what the child looks like from memory, paying attention to hair and eye colour, face shape, teeth, smile, length of hair, the way they usually dress, how they use their hands. Do this in class. As an assignment, have the student build on this description by actually watching the child. Were the two descriptions similar or was there more detail when the student(s) watched their child? Did they see anything they hadn't noticed before? (Describing pets works well, too.)

- Go on a "colour walk". Have each student pick a colour, then go on a walk together with a notebook to write down all the things you see that are of that colour. Come back to the classroom and compare notes. Write about how it felt to look at only one colour in the world around you.

When I Look At You

When I look at you, this is what I see
I see the pain of what used to be.
I look further, deep in your eyes
I see someone who now laughs and also cries.
I see someone with a lot of strength
Someone who will succeed at any length.
I see someone who is willing to share
With a friendly face to show you care.
I see someone who will never forget the past,
But someone who's learned to forgive very fast.
I see someone who has learned from the wrong
I see someone who feels they really belong.
I see someone who has love in her heart
I see someone who has given herself a new start.
When I look at you this is what I see -
I am looking in the mirror at the reflection of me.

Carol
Chapters, Camrose

2. Taste - Mouth

Everyone can identify a favourite taste. Many of us also have memories of terrible tastes and have a list of foods that we prefer not to eat because they "taste bad".

Exercise Ideas

- Have the student(s) describe their favourite "comfort food".

[unedited] My favourite thing before I go to bed at night is a cup of tea and a piece of toast and honey. I love popcorn when I watch TV or am just sitting around in the evening. My favourite dessert is pastry squares but I settle for pumpkin pie because it's cheaper. And I love fries smothered in gravy after a hard day of garage saling.

Sharron
Chapters, Camrose

[unedited] When I need to be comforted I usually turn to ice cream. I think the reason is because it is cold and creamy wet, fills the hunger gap, and helps me feel good because at first it is hard and cold but when you put it in your mouth it melts and just slithers down your throat. Sometimes, when I'm depressed, I wish I could be just like the ice cream and just melt away like it does. But I wouldn't want to ever lose the life I have by being eaten!

Cindy
New Worlds for Women Program, Drumheller

Give the student(s) a list of words and ask them to write a word or a phrase that describes how the item tastes

spinach
chocolate
potato chips
pickles and ice cream

Ask the student(s) to describe the best and the worst thing they ate yesterday, using as many words as possible to describe the tastes.

Use your imagination to describe how things other than food might taste. Write through your sense of taste.

What flavour is your dog?
What would old blue jeans taste like?
What flavour are you?

3. Smell - Nose

Smell is a sense that we don't usually talk about. We say that something smells good or that something smells bad, but we don't talk about smells on a regular basis the way we do about the food we've tasted or the things we've seen. We tend to underestimate how often our olfactory senses can trigger memories or bring us comfort.

Exercise Ideas

A simple exercise is to have the student(s) finish the sentence, "I like the smell of _____ bccausc _____".

[unedited] I like the smell of sweetpeas in a vase in my house because the smell reminds me that sweetpeas were always planted first in my mother's garden. They were her favourite.

Alice
Chapters, Camrose

[unedited] I like the smell of my house after I have cooked or baked. It always seems to hold the smell for a long time and it reminds me of my foster mother because she was always cooking and baking and you could smell it out the windows of the house on the way home from school.

Carol
Chapters, Camrose

Bring in some incense and burn it in the class while you're doing freewriting. Ask the students for their reactions

Do you like this smell?
What does the smell remind you of?
Does burning incense help you to write, or is it distracting?

Have the student(s) write about their favourite perfume or cologne. Most people have a favourite that they wear or that they can identify. Ask what it is about the perfume that they like. There are always articles in women's magazines about perfumes – with descriptions about our personalities matching the scents we wear – such as floral scents for romantics, fruity scents for outgoing types and spicy scents for athletes. This can be fun information to add to a lesson about using your sense of smell.

4. Touch - Hands

As human beings, we need to touch and be touched. We often "see" by touching. We are naturally curious. How often have you wanted to touch the fabric of someone's clothing, just to get a better sense of it and of the person themself? It is unfortunate that society doesn't recognize the importance of our tactile sense, as we continue to put up signs that say "Please Don't Touch".

Exercise Ideas

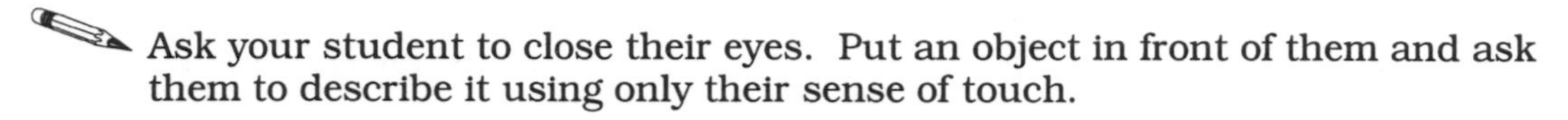

- Ask your student to close their eyes. Put an object in front of them and ask them to describe it using only their sense of touch.

- Have your student(s) describe every kind of texture they can think of – soft, hard, bumpy, scratchy, squishy, slippery.

- Using all the descriptive words you can think of, write a sentence or paragraph to describe

  a tree trunk
  an ice cube
  the sidewalk
  your old blue jeans

5. Sound - Ears

Most of us depend on our ability to see much more than our ability to hear, and yet our world is almost never without sound. As our deaf communities know, communicating without sound is extremely difficult. Imagine how much different our worlds would be without our favourite music to listen to. The trick to hearing well, is learning to listen well.

Exercise Ideas

- Have your students(s) bring in a favourite piece of music. What is it that they like about it? Is it relaxing? Does it lift the spirits? Does the rhythm of the music make you want to dance? Ask your student(s) to describe what music they like to play when they are feeling good.

Go for a walk with your student(s) and find a place to sit quietly. Listen to the sounds around you. What do you hear? Shut out the rest of the world for 5 minutes. You'll be amazed at the sounds you hear that you didn't know were there.

Ask your student(s) to think of someone whose voice appeals to them. What is it about the person's voice they like – perhaps the rhythm, pitch or individuality? Describe someone's laugh. What makes it distinct? Imagine the world without being able to hear laughter. Find a tape recorder and tape your voices. What do you sound like? Use words to describe your voice.

Write about how you feel about sounds. The loud whistle of a train at night is frightening to some people and comforting to others. What sounds are familiar and comforting? Which sounds are jarring or annoying?

Putting it all together

Isolating our senses makes us more aware of them, but in reality, we use all our senses at the same time. Here is an exercise to help students bring all their senses into their writing.

Describe these scenes using all your senses.

a church prayer meeting
a rock concert
a family dinner

Reflections

Our basic English textbooks always said that "good writers use all their senses" to describe scenes or characters. This is true, but *really* good writers also use their senses to understand how they feel, and how they view the world before they begin to write.

We really had our eyes opened in the Chapters classroom when one of the students talked about how different her world was once she quit smoking; she had no idea of all the smells and tastes she had been missing until now. Most of us take our senses for granted; we can't imagine what it would be like not to be able to hear or see. Our senses talk to us. They help us to better appreciate and understand the world around us. Being in tune with our senses means being more in tune with the world.

When I Grow Old
by Sharron

When I grow older I hope to do so many things. I will volunteer in "Chapters" to pass on the experiences I've had and learned from. I will go swimming, ride my bike and walk for miles. I'll put on a huge pot of homemade soup and make fresh bread and chocolate chip cookies. Then I will open my door so that the aroma fills the air. I will sit back in my most comfortable chair and hope someone will stop by and join me for lunch. I'll continue making goodies for all my family and friends. I'll cover coat hangers with wool I picked up at garage sales. I'll give them to anyone that might want them or teach them how to cover them like I learned to long ago. I'll rummage through thrift shops to see what I can buy for a good deal. I like wearing reds and blues and will make things out of what I find that doesn't suit me. I'll pick pussy willows and cover them with chalk. I will play scrabble with my friend if she's still around. I will go to every garage sale within walking distance. Whether it rains, snows or the wind blows, I will dress for the weather accordingly, take my walker and be on my way. I will smile at everyone I meet, hoping they will smile back and think of the days I couldn't smile so easily. Yes, its going to be fun.

(excerpted from Rainbows of Hope*)*

I See, I Feel

What we see and what we feel are not always the same thing. I gave each of my students a picture/photo from *National Geographic* magazine and asked them to write about it. We had been working on using our five senses, so when the students read their work out loud, there were good descriptions of the colours and the details in the pictures. But one of the students surprised us all by writing about how the picture made her feel.

It was a photo of a man in a kayak plunging down a waterfall. Sharron wrote about her fear of heights and how she could never do what the man in the picture was doing because even going down the water slide at the local pool was too frightening for her to even think about. She didn't describe the yellow kayak, the white spray of the waves or the expression on the man's face, she described how the photo made her *feel*.

Sharron's response to this exercise really opened my eyes to the idea of "writing from the heart". When we write about what we see, we "stay on the surface". When we write about what we feel, we are able to get in touch with a much more important level of understanding. Once the students are reawakened to their everyday senses, I use this exercise to help them go one step further and get in touch with their feelings.

Exercise Steps

1. Keep your eyes open for good photographs in magazines or newspapers that have enough detail to catch your attention, but not necessarily to tell the whole story. I keep a file folder of pictures for this exercise and add to it often.

2. Randomly choose a picture from the folder for your student(s). First, ask them to describe what they *see* in the picture, using their five senses as a guide for description.

3. Now ask your student(s) to "switch gears" and write about how the picture makes them *feel*. Does the picture make them feel angry or happy or frustrated? Try to have them identify their feelings, then write about them.

4. Ask each student to hold up the picture they were given. Have them read the description of what they saw in the picture, then the description of how it made them feel.

5. Take time to talk about the difference between seeing and feeling.

Writing Examples

(The pictures the students are describing were taken from *National Geographic* magazines. All pieces are unedited, completed in a five minute writing exercise.)

I see...

I see blue vastness. A lady is prepared to dive or jump from a very high point. She is at a resort of some kind as the area is made up of sand, water, and lush trees. Umbrellas litter the beach causing a village. Sun, sand and sea. There is a big hotel in the peripheral area. The sun is shining.

I feel...

I would be frightened if I was the lady who is taking the plunge at the bungy jump tower. I would feel fight or flight. Risk it all or go on as I have been without doing anything daring.

Barb

Chapters, Camrose

I see...

This is a picture of a llama and a little boy and a woman. The llama is stretching his neck to get close to the little boy who is sitting down on a chair. The little boy is a bit afraid of the llama. He is making a funny face. The llama is being held by the trainer and she is reacting to the llama's curiosity toward the boy. They are in a room with yellow chairs. The llama is more curious about the boy than the boy is about the llama.

I feel...

I can just feel the little boy's nervousness toward this curious animal. I can feel the tension on the boy's part. The trainer knows how to be around the llama which is new to the boy. It makes me laugh to see the boy's reaction.

Alice

Chapters, Camrose

I see...

I see a beautiful blue sky. Scads of geese flying low over what looks to be a field of stubble. Some appear to be swooping down making a landing, maybe it's feeding time. They're all different sizes and mostly greyish white in colour. You can hear the squawking sounds coming from every direction.

I feel...

The picture makes me feel lonely. It reminds me of one big happy family. I want to be up there floating in the clouds. Not a worry in the world.

Sharron
Chapters, Camrose

Adaptations

I enjoy doing this exercise because the students are often surprised (and excited) about the differences they see in their two pieces of writing. I usually do this exercise fairly quickly, allowing about 5-10 minutes for each part simply because I don't want the students to "over think" what they're writing; I just want them to write.

An adaptation of this exercise that works well in a classroom is to have students work in pairs and "swap pictures". Give each of the students a picture, ask them to write about what they see, then have them switch pictures with the person beside them. Now have the students write about how this new picture makes them feel. When the students read their work out loud, one student reads about what they saw in the picture, and their partner reads about the feelings the picture stirred in them. The students are surprised to learn that what they saw or felt in looking at the pictures can be quite different than what others saw or felt.

Reflections

It takes practice to get in touch with our feelings. It didn't take long for the students in the Chapters Program to begin to use their senses to describe "things". They could "stick to the facts" quite easily. Putting facts aside to get to feelings was much more difficult. Once they saw the difference, the students were really keen to do more writing from the heart. They were pleased at their ability to describe and "see" things around them. After years of turning off their feelings, they were now discovering a whole new part of themselves that they wanted to get to know better.

One of the students described her pen and paper as her "friends". She explained that they kept her company as she worked at getting to know herself again.

Oh, and as a footnote, the students were determined that Sharron learn not to be afraid of the water slide at the Camrose pool. After a great deal of encouragement, Sharron finally took the plunge and wrote this poem about her experience.

Conquering Fears

They say life is what you make it
And believe me I know why.
Last night I went swimming
And went down the water slide.
The fear I had within me
I never thought I could
But it's so fun and easy
I only wish you would.
They say to face your fears
And they will go away.
I never did quite understand
Just why it worked that way.
But now that I have tried it
It seems to work for me.
When I went down the water slide
There was one less fear in me.

Anyplace, Anytime

Writing isn't just a classroom activity. In fact, some of the best writing the Chapters students did was while we were on a picnic in the park or sitting in a restaurant having coffee. We got into the habit of always carrying pens and paper with us, just in case something inspired us to write.

Exercise Steps

1. Plan an outing with your student(s). The A&W in Camrose has comfortable booths lined up along-side big sunny windows. It's a perfect place for talking and writing. (And the coffee is good, too!)
2. Take some paper and pens with you.
3. After you are comfortable and have had a chance to catch up on each other's news, do some freewriting together.
4. Refresh your coffee and share your writing with one another.
5. This is a good time to build on an experience by writing about it. Ask the question, "How does it feel to write while you're sitting in a restaurant?" or have your student(s) take a sentence from their freewriting and build on it with more detail and description. Have some other writing ideas along with you in case you would like to do more writing while you are out and about.

Writing Examples

Different But Still the Same

There is a difference
Here in the park
Out of the classroom for a change
Nature together
We are all living breathing beings
   Birds, bugs and people
   Trees, grass and flowers
   Water and pop
   Adults and children
Fine dining out here
Sitting or laying on the grass
We must have a plaid blanket
And a wicker or wooden picnic basket
Slides and swings
Swinging our arms and talking with our hands
New friends we may have just met now together
Celebrating life
Caring about what each other is saying
Listening and tasting the words we are sharing
Blending with nature
Having a picnic
We are making a memory

Patricia
Chapters, Camrose

Adaptations

All writers need stimulation. Outings are great for clearing "writer's block" and for storing ideas for later. We kept an ongoing list on a flip chart of places we wanted to visit. I tried to plan two outings a month, just to keep our energy up. I also found that getting out into the community really helped the students to feel more a part of where they lived. Some didn't know there was an art gallery in Camrose and some had never ventured into the local book store because they thought it was only for "smart people". As a group, we could go anywhere or do anything. We planned our outings (snacks, supplies, etc.) and always looked forward to what we could learn from them. The students tell me now that they.

are more comfortable taking their children on outings, and plan them just as we did in the classroom. Some even take paper and pens – for colouring if nothing else!

The trick with the idea of writing "anyplace, anytime" is to always have paper and pens with you. I travel everywhere with a book bag and always make sure there is a good supply of lined paper in it. The students in Chapters rarely go anywhere now without some sort of writing material – a notebook or scribbler – and they are often the ones to say, "Hey, let's write about this."

Try visiting a local art gallery. Have each student choose a painting that appeals to them and then write about it. If possible, find a place to sit near the painting so that they can look at it as they write. Write about it as a group if possible. Share your thoughts when you get back to class.

There are wonderful places to visit in our communities – the pet shop, the thrift shop, the park (with swings!) or the museum. Make a list of possibilities with your student(s) and plan some special outings.

Reflections

Most outings cost very little, and the rewards can be great. The Chapters students did some typing and layout work for a woman who was putting together a booklet of family stories for which she donated $300 to the Chapters Program. With that money, we decided to go to a bed and breakfast 20 minutes from Camrose. Seven adults and a two year old packed snacks and clothes and stayed overnight in a beautiful log cabin overlooking a lake. We went walking and exploring, stayed up late and talked about our childhoods. In the morning we had a delicious breakfast sitting on the front porch of the cabin. And we did a lot of writing. We wrote about dreams and what it was like to do something you never thought would be possible. We wrote about feeling good and being together as a group. A couple of times I saw the students sitting quietly with their scribblers. They didn't have cameras, but they had words to describe what they saw and how they felt.

We went to galleries and different restaurants (each time a new one opened up we had to go and check it out!), and visited travelling exhibitions and events. When I discovered that many people watched videos at home, but few had been to the movie theatre in Camrose, I encouraged the students to take some of the money they had been raising from selling crafts, to go to the theatre on "cheap Tuesday" to see the movie "Then and Now". The next day the students were anxious to write about how it felt to be in a theatre eating popcorn in the dark. We also wrote about and studied the different characters in the film – what they were like as children and what they were like as adults. We looked closely at the characters to try to understand why they made the choices they did in their lives. I like to call the writing we did in the Chapters Program "Real-Life Literacy". Combining or integrating real life (with occasional flights of fancy) into the classroom helped tremendously with making learning relevant.

Having Fun

Are we having fun yet? By now you will be freewriting and getting used to the idea of "talking on paper" – finding words to express your feelings and thoughts in writing. You should also be feeling comfortable and safe with one another. Congratulations! Now the fun really begins.

This next set of exercises is meant to be fun but challenging too. They will make you think. You may begin to look at life a little differently and you will certainly find that you and your student(s) are getting to know each other better. I can almost guarantee that you will have some good laughs together with these exercises.

Remember to keep a sense of fun alive when approaching these exercises and you will literally be able to watch your students gain confidence as learners and as writers.

Dinner For Two

This is one of my favourite exercises. The idea started with the fact that we all have fantasies about meeting famous people – movie stars, TV characters, authors, or royalty. To get to know my students a little better, I asked them to write about a famous person they would like to have dinner with. They wrote about a wide variety of people – Elvis, Lyle Lovett, Reba McIntyre, Oprah, Shakespeare and Jesus. After using this exercise a few times, I found there was always someone who wrote about someone special to them who wasn't rich or famous. I have now broadened the question, and am always fascinated to hear about my students' dinner guests.

Exercise Steps

1. Ask your student(s) to answer this question in writing:

   "If you could have dinner with anyone in the world, living or not living, who would your dinner guest be, and why?"

   This can be a take home assignment, but spontaneous writing in the classroom always produces honest and more immediate responses.

2. Share your writing with one another.

Writing Examples (all unedited)

I would have dinner with the Queen because I really like the Royal Family, only we would go to McDonalds and I would buy the Queen a Big Mac and we'd eat with our hands and not worry about our manners.

Medicine Hat College Adult Basic Education student

If I could have lunch with anyone
It would be my Great Grandpa
Who died when I was small.
I'd sit and munch and talk with him.
One question I'd ask would be:
What was it like as a boy
All those years ago?
Another:
Why did you marry my Great Grandma?
Another still:
How did you feel when things began to change
From long ago to the time you died?
Things have changed here since then too.
One more thing I'd tell him is:
I love you and miss you lots.

Natalie
Grade 6 student, Camrose

If I could talk to anyone in the world, it would be to Oscar the Grouch. I would ask him:
What makes you so grouchy all the time?
How can you fit all your junk into 1 trash can?
Do you have any friends or relatives you're nice to?
Do you have any special talents?
Where were you born and how old are you?
Are you related to my friend Tina?
Oscar the Grouch has always been my favorite carecter on Sesame Street.

Jill,
Grade 6 student, Camrose

If I could have dinner with someone who's bashfully my hero it would be my Dad. Why is because I never really new him. And the questions I would ask is why he killed himself and what I was like when I was little and what he loved to do. We'd also talk about what my life is now, like I'm going back to school and leaving on my own and that everythings working out fine the one big question would be. Whats it like dieing and is there really life after death. I'd also tell him that I miss him and even though he hurt me so deeply I still love him.

Christina
Fifth on Fifth Youth Services, Lethbridge

If I could have dinner with anyone in the world it would be with my moms real parents. I'd find out the truth about all the lies people said about them. I'd ask them where there other daughter is. That way my mom could meet her sister. I'd ask them to guide my mom through her problems. I think it would be something to meet my grandparents. I'd get to know them and find out how they lived.

Twila
Fifth on Fifth Youth Services, Lethbridge

Adaptations

If you are working one-on-one with a student, you may want to allow time for discussion before the writing activity. Talk about some of your favourite actors or writers, their screen personalities and why you are drawn to them. In a group setting, it is better to have a discussion after the writing activity.

With students who are comfortable with writing, you could lengthen the writing assignment by asking the student(s) to write where they would have dinner and what they would talk about over dinner. These questions are also good discussion ideas to follow this writing exercise.

 Most students are TV watchers and have a favourite show. You might ask them:

"What character on TV do you identify with most, and why?"
"What TV show would you like to be a guest on?"
"What character would you play and what would the scene or show be about?"

Reflections

This is an exercise that can produce really humorous responses at the same time as really sad ones. I added the part of the question that says "living or not living" because many people wrote about family members who had died. As always with "writing from the heart", it is important to validate the students' thoughts and ideas as they're brought forward.

Good Fortune

A friend gave me a box of Chinese fortune cookies when I was laid up in the hospital. (She found them in the specialty section at Safeway for about $3.00.) We had a great time with those cookies; every time I had a visitor we would share the cookies and read our fortunes.

> "You have a keen and active imagination."
> "Children will contribute to your cheerfulness."
> "You will make a fortune with your friend."

As soon as I was back on my feet, I bought a box of fortune cookies and brought them into Chapters. I made some green tea and we had a "good fortune" morning. (I was careful to notice that all the fortunes used in the cookies were positive and pretty generic.)

Exercise Steps

1. Check the Chinese food section of your grocery store to find fortune cookies sold by the box. (Look for green tea, too). If they are not available, the local "Western/Chinese Food Cafe" in your town may be willing to sell or give you a handful of cookies.
2. Give your student(s) a fortune cookie and ask them to read their fortune out loud. (Sometimes the wording is difficult, so have the student tell you what it means in their own words to make sure they have the meaning of the fortune).
3. Have your student(s) take a few minutes to write about what this fortune means to them as individuals. In preparation for writing, ask questions such as,

   - What would it mean in your life if this fortune did come true?
   - Why does/doesn't this fortune mean something to you?

4. Share your writing with one another.

Writing Examples

"Fun and excitement will soon be yours."

Yeah! Is this going to come true? Yes!!! What more can I say? I intend to make fun and excitement central in my life. I seem to have quiet and calm figured out, now its time to explore energy and enthusiasm. I think that, when I was younger, I was afraid of getting into some sort of trouble by having fun and being excited, so I didn't let myself have as much fun as I could have had. But I'm "older" now - more mature - now's the time to "go for it" and live a bigger life.

"Seek to establish your inner sense of serenity"

I'm undergoing a big transition in my life these days. This fortune is one half of this transition. I'll explain.
I believe that, for many years now, my life could be described as outwardly serene and laid-back, but inwardly full of turmoil and yearning.
I intend to switch my inner and outer worlds around.
Outwardly I will seek more excitement and adventure, perhaps making many mistakes in the process, and inwardly I will find a core of peace and serenity.

Terry
Chapters Instructor, Camrose

"Your future will be bright"

Five years from now I dream of being in the "real world". I will be experiencing all the wonderment that the world has to offer. The adventure of exploring places found only in the advertisements. I will be there - in the middle of history, in the exotic places, in the middle of fantasy and between the earth and the sky. I will sing above the pain of the past. I will rise above the fear and only have promises of golden moments. I will be at peace with me. I will know who I am! I will know where I end and the rest of the world begins. There will be treasured moments to share with special people. People who will come into my life and leave a part of themselves in my heart forever.

There will be happiness which will grow from new encounters and a bridge built rather than a wall. I will be whole and feel the real truth of who I am. There will be no more sorrow, only feelings - real feelings - not frozen - my silent screams of pain will turn into joy!

Whitney
Chapters, Camrose

Adaptations

This is not a serious exercise; it's meant to be fun. If you are working one-on-one with a student, you may want to bring out a fortune cookie or two during your coffee break. It may turn into a writing exercise, or it may not. The vocabulary of fortune cookies is often unusual and might be good material for students to add to their word and spelling lists.

Depending on your student(s), this may be a good exercise to use as an opening to talk about different cultures and different traditions. There is much to explore with the Chinese culture. My students really enjoyed learning about how their year of birth was related to an animal – what being born in the Year of the Rat, or the Year of the Monkey meant. (Our local Chinese restaurant has all this information on their paper table mats, which are free to take home after your meal.)

The "Good Fortune" exercise is a handy "extra" to have up your sleeve to add some fun to a lesson.

Reflections

When I did this exercise with my Chapters class, I found that some were believers in fortunes and horoscopes and some were strong skeptics. The skeptics were those who could not see anything positive in their futures (yet) and in fact were afraid even to begin to hope for good fortune because they were sure if they hoped, they would be disappointed.

Those who had the most fun with the exercise were those who had a stronger outlook on life and were able to take the words of the fortune with a grain of salt. It was an eye-opener for me as an instructor to realize how much fear can be attached to the future and how little hope there can be for things to get better.

We ended up having a spirited discussion about horoscopes and psychics and predictions of the future. We talked about the fact that we are in charge of our own destiny and agreed that the choices we make each day are what will ultimately shape our futures.

Terry surfed the World Wide Web on his computer and found this:

Fortune Cookie US invention
(from the "Golden Gater", Jan. 31 95)

After eating in a Chinese restaurant in the United States, diners are accustomed to being presented with a fortune cookie.

These cookies, however, weren't founded in a Chinese bakery. They actually originated in a small Los Angeles bakery in 1919, according to Judge Daniel M. Hanlon's ruling on Oct. 27, 1983, documented in the Court of Historical Review.

After World War I, bakery owner David Jung wanted to give the people he saw in the streets something to eat and a message of encouragement. Jung experimented with different types of batters and methods until he came up with the method used today.

The piece of paper inside the crisp folder wafer is more than a fortune, "It is a philosophy of life," said Nancy Chan, who works for the Golden Gate Fortune Cookies Company in San Francisco's Chinatown.

One must eat the entire Chinese fortune cookie for the fortune on the paper inside to come true, Chan said.

Although the fortune cookie originated in Southern California, Jung was influenced by a Chinese custom. When children were born, families would send out cake rolls with a message inside announcing the birth of the child.

Happiness Is...

Expressing feelings on paper can be difficult. I have found that simple words used to describe feelings are more powerful than lengthier written expressions. I use this very simple exercise to help students begin to trust themselves with writing about their feelings. I have tried this exercise with all age groups and am always pleased with the results.

Exercise Steps

1. Print 4-6 "feeling words" on a sheet of paper or the blackboard, followed by the word "is"

   Happiness is...
   Loneliness is...
   Fear is...
   Change is...
   Love is...
   Hope is...

2. Have the student(s) complete the sentence. Encourage the student(s) to relax and let the words flow instead of thinking too hard or long trying to find the "right" answer. Assure the student(s) that there is no right answer.
3. Share your ideas with one another.
4. If you are working in a group, put all the ideas together and print them out for the students as a simple way of publishing their work. *(see the "Polish and Publish" exercise for more about publishing student writing.)*

Writing Examples

Happiness is... stronger than sadness.
Fear is... not understanding what's happening to me.
Loneliness is... all too familiar.
Change is... something that starts out small and ends up big.
Learning is... joyful and scary work.

(written by members of the Chapters class)

Chapters is...

[unedited] ...very important to me because I have been on welfare for a long time and never saw any hope of getting off until now because as a child I was told I was a very slow learner and nobody made me take education serious because of that and now I am finding I am not a slow learner at all if it wasn't for Chapters I would of never tried to work a computer because I never thought I was capable and didn't want to embarress myself but I feel fine trying new things here because the people in the program don't judge others buy what they can or cannot do.

Carol

Chapters, Camrose

Life Is...

...nice when good things happen to you but it sucks when you don't have a good day.

...different sometimes, fun, sad, happy, angry, but I like life.

...very strange because you can make many choices and you can look back and its weird to think of what might of happened if you made a different decision.

...school. We go to it about 6 hours a day and we sleep about 8 hours a day.

...short and complicated, but it's also a lot of fun because there is so much to do.

...okay. I'm just kind of worried about my marks but I think I'll do ok.

...nifty because you find out a lot of things.

...hard and sometimes not fair. All those bumps and scrapes and bruises.

...neat because everybody is here for a reason, or to accomplish something like world peace or to save someone's life.

(written by members of my son's Grade 6 class)

Adaptations

This exercise is adaptable for all age groups, all situations and all literacy levels. It can be used in writing workshops and classroom settings or with one-to-one tutoring. I have done this exercise with teenagers, elementary school students, academics and my own family.

This is also a good exercise to use in tutor training. It works well as a warm up exercise and can produce quite varied and fascinating results. It works for beginning writers too, as few words are required.

I have also used this exercise to encourage students to think about specific ideas. Instead of using "feeling words", I have put on the board words like:

> Learning is...
> A good job is...
> Being a mother is...

This has been a simple way to get quick but effective responses to an idea.

Reflections

When I did this exercise in the Chapters classroom, I put the collective responses on a flip chart on the classroom wall. Then as we continued our work together, we could add to the list. One day in the spring, one of the students came in on a Monday morning telling the class how much fun she had had going to garage sales on the weekend. She jumped up and grabbed a bright red marker and added to our list "Happiness Is... garage saling!"

The writing that this exercise encourages can provide a collection of thoughts and ideas that can be very powerful for a group. At the end of each of the Chapters publications, the students worked together on a page of collective thoughts on the theme of the publication. "Change is..." from *Butterflies and Bullfrogs*, "Hope is..." from *Rainbows of Hope*, and "...We are Grateful for" from *The Hearts of Women*. Each student could contribute to this page and feel good about the strong statement they were part of, even if they only contributed one line.

My Name

This writing exercise came from a life skills "warm up" I participated in when I took my Life Skills Coaches training at Medicine Hat College. The exercise is called "What's in a name?". We were asked to go around the room and tell the group what our name was and where our name came from. It was really interesting to learn the history behind peoples' names. Some were named after family members, some had names made up of a combination of names. Nick names were brought out (Belle was "Bellybutton", Marsha was "Swampwater"), which provided a good laugh and I found this to be a great way to remember the names of the people in the class.

When I came back to Camrose, I asked the students to tell me the origin of their names. Some didn't know about their own name, but they all had a story to tell about why and how they named their children.

Exercise Steps

1. Ask your student(s) about the origin of their name. If there is a story behind their name, ask them to write about it, to put the story on paper. (Make sure you know the origin of your own name to take part in the exercise.)
2. Share your writing with one another.

Writing Examples

I am happy with the name Carol. It is just a plain, easy to remember name and I think it suits me. I'm glad my name isn't Eve (that's what my mom wanted to name me because my birthday is New Year's Eve).

Although I like my name now, I remember as a small child I wanted to be called Casey very badly and would sometimes introduce myself to other children as Casey and I asked my mom if she would please call my Casey. I don't really know what that was all about. Maybe from Mr. Dressup.

Carol
Chapters, Camrose

I don't know why I was named Hope, but I feel blessed to have such a name. At times I felt that the name Hope was going to be hard to live up to. Now I realize that this is not true. This name means a lot to me for I now believe that there's always hope - no matter what.

Hope
New Worlds for Women, Drumheller

I was named after my mom's teacher. She was always early for school. I was early, too. I wasn't supposed to be born until the end of October but I came at the beginning - in a grain truck. It was harvest time and my mother was driving the truck for my dad. When she told my dad that it was time to go to the hospital, Dad said, "Wait until I am done in the field." Well, I didn't wait. I was born in the cab of the truck. Later, Mom went to the hospital with me, and then back home.

Bonny
New Worlds for Women, Drumheller

Adaptations

A simple exercise for students is to take the first letters of their name and describe themselves. The students can help one another and may enjoy doing this with their children's names as well.

Caring	Participating in Chapters is a pleasure
And	Asking questions is a must for me
Risk taking	Trust in our classroom is comforting
Oh what a	Reactions we are always asked for
Lady	I'm honoured to have been chosen for Chapters
	Chapters has computers, compassion, choices and class
	Icon is a new word in my vocabulary this year
	Attending, awakening - a good combination

Another idea is to have the students write about how they feel about the name they were given. You can also encourage the student(s) to write about the naming of their pets, children or other family members.

Reflections

Many of the students in Chapters didn't know the origin of their names, so I encouraged them to try and find out. A couple of the students were thrilled to learn that they were named after someone important in the family. (Carol always thought she was named Carol because her birthday was close to Christmas, but was fascinated to learn that she was, in fact, named after an old girlfriend of her father's!)

Every name has a story. Some of the students went home after this exercise, and over the supper table made sure that their children knew how and why they were named as they were. Many wrote the stories down so there would be a documented history of the origin of their children's names. They were quite taken with the idea that their own parents would have put as much thought into their names as they did into the names of their own children. Celebrating the name we have is a wonderful way to celebrate ourselves.

Tattoo Parlour

A number of the students in the Chapters Program had tattoos on their bodies. Real ones – elaborate, colourful and distinct. When one of the students said she wished she knew what it felt like to have a tattoo, we got the idea of seeing if we could find some temporary tattoos.

I discovered that San Francisco stores and many drug stores carry packages or strips of temporary tattoos. They are easy to apply and last for a couple of days. I found some packages geared to women, with motifs of hearts, flowers, angels and birds. We had great fun with the tattoos which, as always, produced some great writing.

Exercise Steps

1. Most kids can tell you where to find temporary tattoos. For about $3, you can purchase a package with about 15 large and small tattoos. (This can be another resource to add to your box of ideas for when you need a break or change in routine.)

2. Have the student(s) chose a tattoo and a place to put it. (Yes, you have to do this too!) Help each other apply the tattoos (you will need a cloth and warm water) then take some time for discussion.

   "How does it feel to have a tattoo?"
   "Would you like to have a real one?"
   "What would your family say if you got a tattoo?"
   "Do you know people with a tattoo?"

   (Alice told us a wonderful story of an uncle who had a tattoo of a naked woman on his arm, but as children, all they saw poking out from under the cuff of his long sleeve shirt were the feet, calves and knees of the mysterious woman. It wasn't until they were much older that they were allowed to see what she *really* looked like.)

3. Just for fun, I asked my students the question: "If you were a tattoo, what would you like to be, and where would you like to be put?" You could also have the student(s) write about their feelings about having a tattoo with a question like, "Does having a tattoo make you feel different? Why/why not?"

4. Share your writing with one another.

Writing Examples

[unedited] I would like to be the tattoo of a bracelet Janis Joplin had on her arm. I think she was a tortured soul with many gifts - mystical, you might say. Being on her wrist, I would go wherever she went and meet all the famous musicians she travelled with. I would understand her pain and sorrow and also what brings out her joy. I think it is neat, because with her tattoo, she carried her jewellery to the grave with her even though it was really sad the way she left this world.

Barb
Chapters, Camrose

[unedited] If I were a tattoo, I would like to be a rare purple orchid. I would be unique and I would put it on my own body. Probably on my left arm. It would remind me of something beautiful and unique, very rare. I love purple, whatever shade. I'd look at it and it would remind me of myself. It would not be the beauty of the flower but the uniqueness of it. It would remind me to think of myself not as an object of beauty, but as someone rare and special inside. I think it would pick up my self-esteem to have a tattoo like that.

Alice
Chapters, Camrose

Adaptations

Using tattoos was a good example for me (and the students) of how having fun can turn into creative energy and a great learning experience. The learning doesn't necessarily have to be written about; discussion is often enough. I have found that talking about ideas and feelings (especially in the context of learning) can be just as important and effective as actual hands-on lesson work. Fun exercises such as using tattoos can help build rapport and establish trust with a group and/or instructor. These too are important elements of successful learning.

Sometimes an exercise simply doesn't work the way you had planned – but you'll never know until you try! I've had a few exercises that didn't work as well as I had hoped, but none that was a total failure or waste of time. There is always something to be learned from the effort. And sometimes the learning is more powerful than you ever imagined it would be!

Reflections

I found my own comfort was a little challenged with this exercise, but because a student had suggested the idea, I was willing to be a student myself. It turned out to be a wonderful experience. We laughed and had fun and discovered a great deal about ourselves as women. The students who had permanent tattoos were the encouragers and told stories about when they got their tattoos, and what the experience was like for them.

To my surprise, I learned that the students felt really empowered with a rose tattooed on their arm, shoulder or chest. We crowded into the bathroom and everyone admired their "new looks". Some of the students chose not to participate at first, but were quickly coerced into joining in our fun. A long forgotten feminine and sexual side of the women surfaced and was openly celebrated. Jokes and stories about the tattoos popped up in class for months afterward. And the woman with the permanent tattoos was better understood and openly admired.

Six of the students from the Chapters Program were involved in making presentations at an Alberta Association for Adult Literacy (AAAL) Conference. They each had to get up and speak about their experiences and involvement in the Chapters Program. I brought along some tattoos and an hour before the session (when everyone was feeling especially nervous) we got together in my hotel room and put on a tattoo. I was amazed at the confidence this gave the group. It was their secret, their connection to one another. Their presentation that day was the best ever.

In My Later Years
by Susan

When I am older, I would like to be carefree and spry for my age. I would take long walks and enjoy each day. I would wear purple and sometimes carry balloons in the park. I would smile at everyone I meet and would love to be surrounded by children. I enjoy them because they take you for what you are. I would also blow bubbles down the street. I think that I would enjoy being a lady of eighty.

When I become old, I have no intentions of being a fat lady of eighty. I intend to wear fashionable clothes. By then I will be grey so I intend to use a colour rinse in my hair. Maybe I will sit in a park and feed the ducks with dried bread crumbs. I will also feed the birds in the winter time.

I will also have a cat for a constant companion. It will be a white cat and I will call her Twinkle. She will be as soft as the white clouds in the sky and she will have only love and affection in her eyes for me. Twinkle will meow with contentment when she sees me in the evening. She will sit on my lap and purr while I stroke her and brush her soft fur.

(*excerpted from* Rainbows of Hope)

Taking Risks

All writers feel vulnerable when they write their thoughts and ideas on paper. There they are, in black and white, for all the world to see. People think that putting their thoughts on paper will leave them open to criticism. That's where the trust and comfort you've been working on comes in. Writing from the heart can feel "risky" because it might take your student to a new level of awareness or understanding. But that's not something to be afraid of; its something to celebrate.

Our students may have lived different lives than we have, but their lives are real and interesting and their stories need to be told. Encourage your student(s) to write out loud. Be patient and trust the process; they will write from the heart when they are ready and able to. Share your thoughts with one another. Allow lots of time to talk to and listen to one another. And remember, you are not expected to be a therapist. Trust your intuition and use your common sense. If you feel "in over your head", there are counsellors and agencies available in your community that you can refer your student to.

Favourite Things

Do you have a favourite piece of clothing? Most of us do. Most of us have a handful of favourite things that are important to us and say something about who we are.

When one of the students in Chapters was about to begin a new job, we were helping her to decide what clothes she would need to create a wardrobe for work. This prompted a great discussion about our favourite clothes.

Exercise Steps

1. Do some brainstorming around your old "standby" clothing (the denim skirt that goes with everything), clothes that are comfortable (the purple jogging suit you love but would never want to be seen in), or clothes that make you feel beautiful (the red silk blouse everyone tells you looks wonderful on you).
2. Ask your student(s) to write a story about a favourite piece of clothing. This works well as an in-class or homework assignment.
3. Share your writing with each other.

Writing Examples

I have a favourite piece of clothing that I love very much. It is my high-top runners. I wear them every day and would feel funny if I didn't. A pair lasts me about a year and every time I get a new pair I get them pretty much the same as the last ones. I have been wearing these types of shoes for about fifteen years - because ever since my legs grew so long high-tops can hide the fact that my pants are always too short. I have tried many other types of runners when it's time to buy a new pair, but after trying on a few dozen, I just know I won't be comfortable in them and go back to my high-tops. Somehow my high-tops give me a sense of security and I don't think I'll ever give them up. I hope by the time I'm an old woman, Adidas will have invented a pair of orthopedic high-tops for me.

Carol
Chapters, Camrose

Adaptations

This exercise made me think of the words from a song from the Sound of Music: *"These are a few of my favourite things"*. Talk to your student(s) about their favourite things. If you are in a group, make a list. Here are some ideas to help you write about your favourite things:

- If you could put all your most important and favourite treasures into a time capsule that would be opened by your family 100 years from now, what would you want to make sure is in there?

- What's your favourite thing to eat?

  [unedited] Well, my fav. food. Well let's see. I'll start with desert. I like donuts prefereing choclate long jons. Food I'm not that picky about is fast food such as fries hamburgers stuff like that. Drinks, I can't drink beer with my meals its just gross. Maybe a pop or juice I don't no I guess that's it.

  Dayna
  Fifth on Fifth Youth Services, Lethbridge

- What favourite things do you think you would like to pass onto your children?

- What is the most inexpensive but precious thing you own?

  When my son was six years old, he gave me a fragile, blue robin's egg for Mother's Day. It is one of my greatest treasures.

  Deborah
  Chapters Instructor, Camrose

- Most "favourite things" have a story behind them. Ask your student(s) to describe a favourite thing and explain why it is important to them. Tell us the story.

My Most Prized Possession
by Maureen

I would say my most prized possession is my coffee table. My coffee table is just wonderful. It's always cluttered with paper, cigarette rolling stuff, an ashtray, a pen and a remote control. I didn't have my table for a few weeks when I moved and wow, was it ever missed. Using an upside-down cardboard box just doesn't cut it.

My table allows me to set my glass, or occasionally my plate on it. Sometimes I put my feet up on it. I write notes on it. I've sat on it and even danced on it a long time ago. It held up my friends' and my family's drinks. It held up baby bottles and toys, books and purses. It supported my girls when they were learning to walk. It may not be exquisite but it serves many purposes.

You may wonder why a crooked and worn coffee table is prized. It is not its looks that make it valuable to me. Reggie, a good friend, used to make and sell coffee, end and kitchen tables. I helped him by holding things, fetching, sanding, filling in cracks, torching and varnishing. He gave me a coffee table and end table for helping him. This was about 14 years ago. He was a true friend who helped me believe in myself. He died a few years back and part of him is in the things he made, so I'm glad I always have a part of him near me.

(*excerpted from* Butterflies & Bullfrogs)

Reflections

A couple of my students wrote about not liking anything in their wardrobes, or having lost or "left behind" an old favourite when they had to leave an abusive situation suddenly. We all decided that we need clothes that make us feel good, so the class took a trip to the local thrift shop the next day. We had a wonderful and inexpensive morning trying on all kinds of things, each of us coming home with a new find. We also decided to clean out our cupboards and have a "clothing exchange" at Chapters. Barb got the clothes she needed for her work wardrobe, we "spring-cleaned" our cupboards and we did some great writing.

I asked the students to write about how it felt to buy something new for themselves (many felt shy about treating themselves). We wrote about how it felt to share with and help one another. The students talked about how others often judged them by their appearance; they were interested to learn that even though I have nice clothes, I experienced many of the same fears and uncertainties about the way I dress. We had great discussions about style and what really makes a person an individual.

Once the students got a good sense of each others' tastes and styles, the clothing exchange and visits to the Thrift Shop and church rummage sales continued with amazing results. I have always worn long skirts, but not any more! One of the students came into class one day with a short denim jumper that has become a real favourite of mine. I did some writing myself about how it felt to try a new style. When I read it to the class they applauded and are now quick to remind me that it's been awhile since I wore something a little shorter! All of this, from a simple writing exercise about a favourite piece of clothing.

Thrift Shop Therapy
by Patricia

There is a place where I can go
Where no one bothers me,
It is my family thrift store
Its all the therapy I need.
It doesn't usually cost much, but
You can't imagine how good
it makes me feel.
I really enjoy my purchases, because
They're almost free.
There are many friends I've made there
Who accept me for who I am.
They are very kind to me, and
They don't question me to death.
I thank all those generous people
Who donate such wonderful things,
because
All of this money goes back
into our community.
So think twice before you
throw that junk away
This place will take it willingly
In our community, it is a necessity.
This is how I get feeling good about me
And I call it thrift shop therapy!

(*excerpted from* The Hearts of Women)

Key Ideas

I found a brown cardboard cigar box of my grandfather's, full of antique keys. There were skeleton keys and trunk keys and keys for winding clocks. I was so intrigued by the collection that I took it into the classroom to show my students. I hadn't planned to use the keys in a writing exercise until Shelly picked up a key and said, "Just imagine what door this key might have opened". There was immediate excitement – "Maybe a door to a boudoir...", "I bet it opened a door to an old cellar...", "Maybe this is the key to a treasure chest!" The students were having such fun with the possibilities, it seemed like a perfect time to sit down and do some writing.

Exercise Steps

1. See if you can find some old keys. Ask friends or relatives if they have some or watch for them at flea markets and garage sales. Most of us have keys in the backs of drawers that no longer have a use. Brand-new, shiny keys would work as well.

2. Bring the keys to your learning setting. Encourage the student(s) to choose a key. Hold the keys in your hands as you talk about all the possible uses keys have. You can talk about the time you locked your keys in the car or the time you dropped your key down the sewer grate. And you can talk about what it means to be able to open something, how it feels after a long day to come home and unlock the front door of your home. After some discussion, it's time to write.

3. Referring to the key the student is holding, ask the question:

   "If this key could open any door, what would that door be?"

4. Share your writing with one another.

The Door to Peace

If I had a key to open any door, it would be the door to peace. Behind this door there would be no war, no starvation, no anger no stress, no heartache, no loneliness, only a calm, quiet serenity that is peace. As I slowly walk through the doorway of peace, I would feel the fear, the loneliness, the anxiety and the frustration start to float away. At first it would be a strange sensation and I would not really be sure of what was happening. I would wonder if I should go on. I would be confused as I stood there. But then I would go on, because the strange sensation would not scare me. Instead it would intrigue and entice me. I would continue on until I came to the centre of that peaceful place. I would look, listen, and hear the joy that would be surrounding me. I would wonder why we do not all journey through the wonderful doorway to peace, so that we may all be at peace together as well as all be at peace alone.

There would be one time that I would venture back to the door, but only to leave the key in the lock for those who would like to enter, but seem unable to find their key. My key is for you, please join me in peace.

Norma

Basic Job Readiness Training, Medicine Hat

The Key To My Heart

I wear this key so close to home
And fondly touch it wherever I roam

It brings fond memories once again
Of joy, of sorrow, of love, and pain

A lock of hair from my first horse
My first grade reader and chalk of course

A locket given to me at birth
Within, my parents smile in mirth

My precious doll, we named her Margo
Along with my picture of the old Fargo

Within that truck my parents were wed
My brother was carried, travelled, and fed

The rice picture I so carefully did
The flowers I pressed and loved and hid

Some rocks that I dug, cherished and saved
That one summer, we travelled with spade

The pictures of my very first wedding
So young and so happy, so loving, so giving

The skirt that my mother wore in her youth
That I'd hoped to wear, just like her, in truth

The picture of me, on my Daddy's knee
Left foot over right knee, me in between

My grandmother's chair-cover,
in many bright colors,
The woman I loved above all others

May I always remember to fondle this key
That opens the trunk of my memory

To carry me back to the things that I loved
To the people who live and to those up above.

Sheilah
Chapters, Camrose

[unedited] If this key could open any door, it would open the door to my happiness. This would allow me the freedom to trust others and to believe once again (like I used to) that people out there aren't just out for themselves. I used to believe that, and was a much happier person. I'd like to somehow believe that again. Maybe I was naive back then, but I'd still like to believe that there's some good in this world.

Michele
Fifth on Fifth Youth Services, Lethbridge

Adaptations

The question you have asked your student(s) is a simple one. Depending on the comfort level of the student(s), you could take the idea further and ask:

"If this key could open anything, what would it be?" (This question is broader and may give the student more room to use their imagination).

[unedited] If this key could unlock something, it would be the thoughts that are going through my son's mind because right now I really wish I knew what was going through his mind. I would really like him to talk to me and tell Mommy what's a matter so I can help but he won't. I know he's only six years old but he's going through a lot. I want my little boy back. I love him so much and I really wish this key could open up the thoughts he is having.

Patty
Chapters, Camrose

An even more powerful question is:

"If this key could *lock* any door, what door would that be?"

This question may be especially challenging as students might choose to write about sad or difficult things in their lives they would like to lock away.

I have tried this exercise with students of all levels, and with instructors as well. "Key Ideas" would also be a good tutor training warmup when teaching about the writing process. The variety of writing that comes out of a group setting can lead to terrific discussion and to the realization that we all have different ideas and approaches to questions in life.

Reflections

I was amazed by the response I got to this exercise. The students' imaginations were wonderful, and so were their different approaches to the question. Some wrote about the key to peace, to freedom or to the end of poverty. Some wrote about finding a long-lost family member on the other side of the door, and one student wrote a poignant story about locking the abusive life she had behind a door, then throwing the key into a river.

Each of the stories students wrote using this key exercise talked about things that were important to them – a grandmother's trunk that came over from the old country to Canada, a door to a new house that is fully paid for, a hope for children living in poverty. These are strong values. This exercise will help you and your student(s) to understand a little more about what you value and what is important to you.

I was so moved by the students' stories and how taken they were with my grandfather's old keys that I bought some inexpensive ribbon and tied a key to the ribbon so that each of the students could wear one around their necks. They saw the keys as keys to possibilities and good things, and wore them regularly.

Going to School at 52!
by Patricia

Going to school at 52
Often feel like I don't have a clue
And probably don't...
But... someone was willing to give me a chance
I will be forever grateful
It's such a good feeling
When you find you are learning
Some of what you already know
From the heart
Locked away
What we thought were endings
Are really new beginnings
New opportunities and the hope
That we really can do great
Things
That are important.
We really are worth a great deal
As individuals and as women
Because life is a "big deal"
Learning is a valuable and essential asset...
Every day I'm given 24 hours and I get
To choose what to do with them.
(excerpted from Rainbows of Hope)

Looking Back

Most of the adults in our programs, if not all, have come through difficult times. For some, the wisdom they have gained through their experiences has lead them to our programs. They want to make changes. They are ready to learn and in many cases, are excited about the idea of learning.

I often heard my students say, "I sure wish I knew then what I know now". They talked about knowing now that if they hadn't dropped out of school, maybe finding work wouldn't have been so hard, or if they hadn't gotten married so young, they might have had a chance to see more of the world. One of the students talked about what she would like to teach her daughters, given her own life experience. She didn't want them to go through what she did. We turned her thoughts into a writing exercise for everyone in the class.

Exercise Steps

1. This is an exercise that benefits from brainstorming or initial discussion. Talk about some important things you and your student(s) have learned over the years. Try to focus the discussion on positive learning, not just "regrets" or "mistakes".

2. Ask the student(s) to respond in writing to one of these questions:

    "What do you know now, that you wish you knew when you were younger?"
    "Given your life experiences, what advice would you give an 18 year old boy/girl?"

3. Read your writing out loud to one another.

Writing Examples

[unedited] I would say, Be who you are. I wish somebody had said that to me. Cherish the good things you are and love the bad til it goes away. Every living, breathing person is here for a reason. They have a purpose. Explore who you are. Write things down to record a history for yourself. It might be a great guideline for an award winning novel. Be aware of your surroundings. Rejoice in the moment. Have great moments. Take time to savor them. Use your memory for good things, don't dwell on the bad. Deal with things as they come. Work at being invincible spiritually. Stand for something. Dare to love.

Barb
Chapters, Camrose

[unedited] I wish at 18 I would of believed in myself more. I wish I would of believed that even though I was a mother already, I still could go back to school and do whatever I wanted to do. I remember I really wanted to be a nurse but I probably would be unemployed right now due to cutbacks! I also would of liked to be able to solve problems better and would of liked to no how to make good choices for myself.

Carol
Chapters, Camrose

[unedited] I know today that I am alot smarter than I ever thought I was then. I know that anything is possible if you want it and that no one is to dumb to learn or be what they would like to become. I always thought I had to do everything and anything I was told to do. I also know there is only one me and that if I had taken better care of me when I was 18, I would maybe, just maybe, be in the workforce today enjoying life more and feeling better.

Sharron
Chapters, Camrose

[unedited] The fears you feel now, the reasons you hesitate to do the things you wished you could do, aren't as big as you think they are. In a few years, you'll look back and say 'I wish I'd have taken the chance and...' Its normal to feel afraid to take risks, but you'll feel good about yourself if you bravely take them anyway. If things go wrong, years later maybe you'll laugh about your youthful mistakes. If things go right, well, you're that much further ahead.

Terry

Chapters Instructor, Camrose

Adaptations

"Looking Back" is not an exercise for everyone. It is best used with students who are are relatively comfortable with themselves and not still "stuck" in the past. This exercise is a good starting point for discussions about learning and growing and becoming who you want to be. Students are quick to see events in their past as mistakes, not something they can learn from. After a really good discussion about looking at the good that had come from some difficult situations, one of my students told me that she had decided: "If you make a mistake and learn from it, then it was a learning experience. But if you make a mistake and don't learn from it, it will always be a mistake." She also decided for herself that sometimes you have to repeat a mistake three or four times before you actually learn from it.

I have used this exercise to help students see the value of their pasts, to understand that even though they can't change the past, they can learn from it and make good choices for themselves based on that learning.

Reflections

My heart aches when students talk about their pasts and the trials and sometimes horrors they have been through. They seem to understand that the past is not something they can change, but learning to live with the past is something else again. Seeing the value of their past experiences helps tremendously with their ability to move forward in their learning and in their lives. I always try to balance discussions about the past with memories of good things that have happened. It too often seems easier for students to focus on negative events instead of what is good. Sometimes as instructors, we are able to help students rethink past experiences so that the events can be thought of in a more positive light.

It is important to encourage students to look and think "forward" in their learning, but it is sometimes helpful (and even necessary) to look back to see what the roadblocks to learning have been. In literacy programs, students don't just "learn to write". If given the opportunity, they can also "write to learn". Thinking about events through writing helps tremendously with the process of building confidence and moving forward in life.

Children

Life is precious; take time for your family, especially your children. I have always been a working person. When my children were killed in a car accident in 1981, I realised how much of their lives I had missed, always putting things before them.

I would go to work and kiss them goodbye, thinking that everything would be alright. Then one day, it wasn't. God took over my job as a parent. In His infinite wisdom, He took my children to live with Him forever.

Do not, under any circumstance, ever put anything or anyone ahead of your family or children. You don't know how long you will have with each other.

Children are the greatest gifts God gives; but they're ours for only a short time.

Money and material possessions are of absolutely no consequence, if you are alone.

Lynn
Secretarial Refresher Program, Drumheller

Friends & Companions

Most of us have a best friend or at least a really close friend. When I began to ask questions in the classroom about what makes someone special to us, one of the students said, "It's been so long since I had a good friend, I don't think I know what that means anymore." We decided it was important to refresh our memories about friendship and why certain people are particularly important to us.

Exercise Steps

1. Talk to your student(s) about friends they now have, or have had in the past who have been important to them. List memorable characteristics about the person. List qualities in people that we all admire and respect.
2. Have the student(s) write about a former or current friend. To encourage writing, ask the student(s) questions like:

   "What makes this person special?"
   "How do you feel when you are around them?"
   "How did you become friends in the first place?"

[unedited] I have a best friend her name is Stephanie she is cool I have Known her since grade 4. We did everthing together. I like her so much because I can trust her with my secrets. And she knows that she can trust me too. We used to have such fun together. That was until I moved from Calgary. But we still talk all the time I phone her she phones me to.

Jennifer
Fifth on Fifth Youth Services, Lethbridge

[unedited] What I like about my friend Brett is that he's helped me through so much and when I need to talk to someone he's always there and even though we may drink together he always takes care of me so I don't make a fool of myself. We also have went out before and it really hasn't afected our relationship. Anyway, he's caring thoughtful and very sweet that's why he's my very close friend.

Christina
Fifth on Fifth Youth Services, Lethbridge

[unedited] I think my Best friend Kylene is special because she always calls me, we do a lot of things together, we even have a secret language that no one understands. We always Know what each of us is going to say or thinking, we have best friend rings and got the same tattoo together to represent our friendship. I think shes cool because she always know when somethings wrong and always says nice things.

Brandi
Fifth on Fifth Youth Services, Lethbridge

3. Now, have some fun and ask the student(s) thc following question:

   "If you were shipwrecked with a total stranger on a desert island for one month, what would you want that person to be like?"

4. Share your writing with one another.

Writing Examples

[unedited] I would have to say after thinking about this for over an hour and a half that I would want to have my son Matthew with me. To spend months with nothing to do except being with him teaching him all the things that I want to. Playing and singing with him would be absolutely wonderfull. He is there when I would need a hug or kiss and just watching him learn and grow without any other distractions would be wonderfull.
I would teach him to sing songs, paint, colour, have conversation

with him. Another way it would be nice is that I wouldn't have to deal with an adult's moods and quirks. No demands except those that I could deal with already.

April
Chapters, Camrose

[unedited] I think the most important quality my companion would have is the ability to talk with me about anything. I think life on this island might be rather stressful, and if there wasn't some way to cope with the inevitable tensions and conflict, things would get bad fast. Being able to talk (and listen) means they need to be trustworthy and respectful. I would need to feel that my companion really cared about me, would never want to see me hurt and knew that my thoughts and feelings mattered.
Of course, it would really help if my companion was funny and interesting and adventurous. Life on this island could even be fun, if we let it be.

Terry
Chapters Instructor, Camrose

1) has a fishing rod and a fridge full of food
2) doesn't snore
3) easy to start conversations with and keep the conversation going
4) an extraverted person
5) strong but smart
6) can cheer up a swatted fly
7) likes attention
8) can stand being around me for a month
9) tells me when he or she needs help
10) has lots of ideas
11) an outdoors person
12) a good cook
13) an explorer
14) fun person with a sense of humour

Josh
Deborah's son, age 11

Adaptations

A low-level student may want to simply look at and study the words around the characteristics of a good friend – words such as "patient", "generous", "knowledgeable" or more simply "caring", "kind" or "fun". Look the words up in the dictionary. Practice spelling them.

In a comfortable group, you could have the student(s) write about or describe their perfect companion. Ask your student(s) to respond to the question:

> "How would you describe the person who would be your perfect male or female companion?"

Students may choose to write a letter to the friend (current or in the past) and tell them how much their friendship has meant. The letter does not have to be mailed, but it can be very powerful for the student to use words to express gratitude to a friend. Exercises like this have lead to letter exchanges and phone calls from people the students hadn't heard from in years.

Reflections

Friends are important to us all. I learned that not all of us are lucky enough to have good friends that we can turn to or count on. Many of my students talked about how they always seemed to end up with friends who were not honest, took advantage of them or ended up hurting them. With a little more digging, we were each able to find at least one person who had truly been a friend.

We talked about how we can sometimes attract people who are not good for us and why this happens, but we also talked about friends who had seen us through hard times and who could make us laugh when no one else could.

Again, I needed to remember that life for many of my students is difficult (and has been difficult in the past) because of disappointing and unhealthy relationships, often with people they thought were friends.

Good friendships *are* possible. "Friends and Companions" helped the students re-identify why friends are important. It also helped them think about what qualities they like in others and who their good friends really are. After doing the exercise, one of the students said, "Now I think I'll know better what to look for when I'm meeting new people."

Things I Miss

I often heard the students talk about things they missed now that their lives were taking a different turn. (There were also many things they *didn't* miss.) The age of the students in my class ranged from 20 to 53 years, but many of the students missed similar things – closeness, touch, friends, family and lost belongings. It was interesting that as they started talking about things they missed, they were also able to help each other think and write about what they could do to lessen their feelings of loss.

Exercise Steps

1. I like doing this exercise without brainstorming or prewriting exercises because I found more immediate responses came from the students when they didn't think too much about it beforehand.
2. Ask the student(s) to write about what they miss.

   "What do you miss that you used to do when you were a child?"
   "What fashions do you miss that used to be popular?"
   "What do you miss about not being with your family?"

3. Share your writing with one another.

Writing Examples

[unedited] I miss having a family get together with roast chicken on a Sunday afternoon. Today meals are just an everyday thing and everyone is just too busy to get together.

Barb
Chapters, Camrose

[unedited] I miss the chocolate bar that was called Wig Wag. I remember the commercial that used to say "Wig Wag, it's 2 hands high". Then it showed 2 kids hanging on to it. I remember when I would get money for the store I would buy one because it was the biggest chocolate bar you could get.

Hey, I know what else I miss. Whatever happened to the Pep Chew? And blue Koolaid? I really used to enjoy blue Koolaid. Maybe I should write to Koolaid and ask them! Yes, that's it, I'll start a petition to bring back the blue Koolaid!

Carol

Chapters, Camrose

Adaptations

As the instructor, you will have a good sense of what your student(s) can handle. If you are working with an ESL student, you may want to talk about what the student misses from their homeland. It might be possible to find an ethnic community near you that sells foods that are familiar to the student or help them connect with other people from the same country.

If you are working with a group, you may find that many of the students miss similar things. One of my students wrote about missing colouring with pastels that were given to her when she was little. Others remembered what pastels felt like (unlike crayons or felt pens) so I brought in a box of pastels from home. We drew pictures then wrote about how it felt to do something as a grown up that we used to do as children.

If you have a strong relationship with your student(s) you may want to write about things the students don't miss.

> "I don't miss having to share all my clothes with my sisters."
> "I don't miss feeling like I wasn't worth anything when my family was on welfare."

This is certainly more difficult memory writing, but it can be also be very helpful for the student to "get it out", and it will help you to get to know more about your student(s).

Reflections

We can all think of things we miss, but we tend to forget that many of the things we miss are things that aren't necessarily gone forever. Terry wrote this with the class:

> *I think all boiled down, I miss the experience of childhood. Material things come and go in fashion - what's no longer around might be back someday. But riding my bicycle to the empty lots on the outskirts of town with my friends is not ever going to happen again. Or is it? I still have a bike, I still have friends, there are still interesting places to ride to...*

Barb talked about Sunday dinners and everyone being too busy these days to get together. Maybe it's still possible to arrange a Sunday dinner, perhaps once a month instead of every week. Carol was really pleased when she discovered blue "Crush" at Safeway, which she said was almost as good as blue Koolaid.

Writing about the little things, the aesthetic memories we have from childhood or from good times in our lives, helps us to identify what makes us feel good, what makes us happy. I have learned through writing about "Things I Miss" with my students, that there are many things we miss that are still possible. Finding ways to replace some of those things can bring hope and new energy to our lives.

What I Know For Sure

I didn't know my students well when Chapters first started. To try to get a better sense of their plans for the future, I asked them to write about where they hoped to be five years from now. I learned a lot from their responses, but not what I had expected to learn.

Most of the students said they could barely imagine where they would be tomorrow, let alone five years from now. Their needs were so immediate; thinking about the future was frightening and unrealistic for them. Trying to listen and understand, I then asked them to tell me what they knew for sure. "What are the things that you can count on, that you know in your heart will still exist past tomorrow?" This exercise took some thought, but it helped us all put aside our fears and focus on things we were sure of.

Exercise Steps

1. This is best done as a homework assignment, but some brainstorming around the idea is still important. Talk to your student(s) about what is known and what is unknown. We know what happened in the past, but we don't know what the future holds.

   What do we know will happen each day?
   Do we have any control over what happens each day?
   How much are we able to influence the events of the day, and how much is simply "chance"?

   Even though the future is unpredictable, there are some things we know for sure. We know that the sun will rise every day (even though we can't always see it) and that a part of the 24 hours of the day will be night. What else do we know for sure?

2. After brainstorming (and hopefully some good discussion) ask your student(s) to write a list of five things they know for sure.

3. Share your writing with one another.

Writing Examples

I know for sure I love my kids.
I know for sure I don't want to end up like my mother.
I know for sure that alcohol can ruin a family.
I know for sure that someday I'm going to die.
I know for sure that I will always have these stick out ears.

Chapters in-class writing

This I Know For Sure

The sky is going to be sunny
Things are going to be funny
We will laugh, we will cry
As every day goes by
This I know for sure.
I know the grass isn't always green
Things aren't always what they seem
There's going to be better things ahead
as we travel on
Sometimes the ground isn't going to be easy
to tread upon
As every day goes by
This I know for sure.
There's going to be war and violence
None of it is going to make any sense
There's going to be promises broken
Between individuals harsh words will be spoken
As every day goes by
This I know for sure.

Marie
Chapters, Camrose

Adaptations

If you have had some good discussion around these questions, you may want to ask your student(s) to elaborate on one thought instead of making an extended list. To have the student take their thoughts and writing a step further, you can ask questions such as:

"Why do you know this for sure?"

Reflections

I have learned so much about real life and about myself through working with the students in the Chapters Program. I took so much for granted. When a person's most pressing concerns are food and shelter, it only makes sense that thinking about the future (especially in a positive light) would be difficult. As instructors, our students often think we are privileged, that our futures are much brighter than theirs will ever be. This may certainly be true, but all of us have had times in our lives when the future wasn't bright, when we were scared, when the unpredictability of events caused us to lose our faith and our hope. We need to remind ourselves of those times to be able to empathize with our students. We also need to think about how we survived those times and how we have come to expect change and unpredictability and how we now see change as a challenge that can be quite exhilarating. We need to help our students regain or build a sense of hope. Without hope, the future can seem pretty bleak.

This exercise was hard work (for me too) but it was the beginning of a lot of work we did around the idea of hope and planning and taking back our personal power. I continually build my thinking around the ideas of what I know for sure. It's a safe place to start. I am pleased to tell you that most of the Chapters students were eventually able to take the risk of thinking forward to the future and, in fact, are now looking forward to what the future holds for them.

The Next Ten Years
by Carol

In the next ten years I plan to eat more fruit – exotic fruit like papayas, and mangoes. I'm going to quit buying plain old apples and oranges. I'd also like to buy all different kinds of cheeses, ten different kinds at once and have fruit and cheese trays daily with all different sorts of crackers.

I would also like to change my hairstyle and put a colour in it. I really really want to stop chewing my nails and I would like to stop bossing my little sister around and stop worrying about her all the time.

I would like to stop smoking and when I do I am going to put a "No Smoking" sign right on my front door.

I would like to get a cat, but not just any cat. I want one that as soon as I see it, I just know I really love it – like my old cat Piper who I miss dearly.

Of course I am going to finish school and have a great job and hopefully in ten years, I will have put away enough money for a deposit on a house. Sara and Daniel will be in college having a great time and Laura will still be at home saying, "I wish I was the oldest. I wish I was in college, too."

(excerpted from The Hearts of Women*)*

Building Confidence

When we feel confident about our ability to learn, our desire to learn increases. I watched the students in Chapters come to a point of wanting to know how to spell a word in a sentence they were writing. They knew that they could write the sentence; now they wanted to write it "better".

It is exciting for the students to look back at their freewriting and see how much their writing, thinking and self-expression have improved. They see how much they have grown in their personal lives and how much more they understand the world around them. They recognize that they have become much better readers, through reading their work out loud and in finding new interest in books and information. They have learned to use a computer, have worked as a team to solve problems and have begun to laugh again. They can now see themselves as competent learners and suddenly find themselves wanting, even needing, to learn more.

Some people say that people gain confidence once they learn new skills; I would argue that once confidence (or faith in oneself) is established, new skills are learned with greater commitment and energy.

Character Development

To give the students a break from writing about themselves or people and places they were familiar with, I had everyone develop imaginary characters. Even famous writers admit that creating imaginary but lifelike characters can be difficult. To ease the process and get the ball rolling, I gave the students some "hints" about the character I wanted them to develop.

On index cards, I wrote the age and sex of the character along with two personality traits or details. The students drew cards, then created and wrote about weird and wonderful imaginary people.

Exercise Steps

1. Prepare index cards ahead of time. (I always prepare more cards than there are students so that the students have lots of choices, especially for those who are the last to pick a card.) Have fun and vary the details as much as possible.

   Example: 23-year-old man, university student, shy and quiet
   46-year-old woman, divorced with three kids, successful trucker
   19-year-old man, negative attitude, wants to travel

2. Have each student pick a card. If possible, don't talk about what's on the card. Encourage the student(s) not to think too much about the details, but to just let their imaginations go. Here are some suggestions for developing the character.

   What is the character's name?

   Where did she grow up? How many kids are in her family? Is she the baby or the oldest child?

   Does he work? What job does he do? Does he like his job or would he like to change careers?

   What are her hobbies? What does she do on weekends? What makes her tick?

   What are his hopes for the future?

3. Introduce the characters to one another by reading about them out loud. Have the students read the information on the index card, then their detailed writing about the character.

Writing Examples

25-year-old woman, risk taker, wants a relationship

[unedited] Marilyn is lost in her thoughts today. She is going on her first blind date. She has never been on one. She has never had to be "fixed up" before. Men have always come to her, but she hasn't had a date for 2 years.

Her last relationship left her with a bad taste in her mouth. Her relationship with Bob was very controlling. They lived together for 6 months and he abused her. Drinking and stealing and getting into trouble with the law. She should have known, but she was blinded by this smooth talking, handsome man on a Harley Davidson motorcycle. She isn't sure about this blind date after being with Bob.

Her friend Suzie says it's time. Marilyn has collywobbles in her stomach. It's the first step to getting over Bob. The pain is gone, but her memories of the abuse are still in the back of her mind. But she knows, like Suzie says, it's time to move ahead.

Alice
Chapters, Camrose

80-year-old woman, serene, ready to die

[unedited] Eva's days are all pretty similar these days. Occasionally she gets visits from her children and grandchildren, and sometimes the lodge arranges little day trips for her and her neighbours to the mall or the greenhouse, but normally she spends her days cleaning her apartment or knitting and making little gifts for her family.

She has everything she needs and often thinks fondly of how happy her family is and how content she has become with what she has accomplished in her long life. The one negative thing she sometimes feels is loneliness. Her husband, Roman, died more than ten years ago and her brothers and friends have all passed on as well. She is happy with her family's occasional visits and would rather have them enjoy their busy lives than spend any more time with her.

Eva's health is not the best since her fall last spring, but she's not too concerned. She is looking forward to reuniting with Roman when she gets to Heaven.

Terry
Chapters Instructor, Camrose

40-year-old woman, going back to school, shy and withdrawn

[unedited] Hi, my name is Holly. I have lived on a farm all my life up until 2 months ago. I just left an abusive marriage and moved to the city. I have always known that I would leave my husband but I wanted to wait until my kids were grown. I don't know if I did anyone any favours by doing this.

Now I am in the city by myself. To someone else this may not be a big deal, but to me it is like being in a foreign country. I wonder if it will ever feel like home here. I long for the feeling to belong somewhere. I am going to go back to school and see how that goes. I feel very nervous about meeting new people but at the same time, i want to start my new life. I think about what crises really means. Dangerous, opportunity, being scared. I know I have to take some risks if I'm going to make this work.

Carol
Chapters, Camrose

Adaptations

The above writing samples were done in about ten minutes of class time with very little preparation. This could also be a good homework assignment. You and your student(s) could develop a set of questions that would help with developing the character in more detail.

A new writer may enjoy developing the character with the tutor acting as the scribe. The finished characterization could be used as reading practice for the student, with identified words being used for vocabulary and spelling practice.

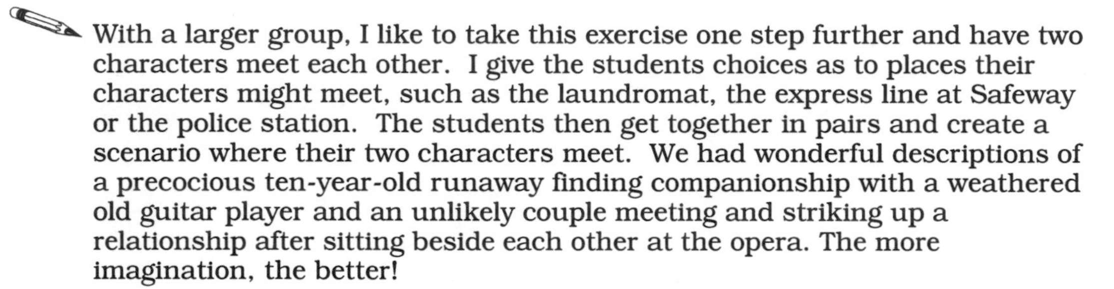

With a larger group, I like to take this exercise one step further and have two characters meet each other. I give the students choices as to places their characters might meet, such as the laundromat, the express line at Safeway or the police station. The students then get together in pairs and create a scenario where their two characters meet. We had wonderful descriptions of a precocious ten-year-old runaway finding companionship with a weathered old guitar player and an unlikely couple meeting and striking up a relationship after sitting beside each other at the opera. The more imagination, the better!

Another idea I would like to try is to come back to the characters a month or two later to write about where they are now. How was Marilyn's date? What does Holly study when she goes back to school? Did Eva die and find Roman? Building on the individual characters could develop into a terrific short story over a period of time. Even as I was putting this lesson together for this handbook, Terry saw his writing again and said with a real fondness, "Oh yeah, I remember Eva."

Reflections

This kind of writing would have been very difficult for my students when they first came to Chapters. They were not prepared to take risks with their imaginations or with their ability to write. When the time was right, however, they really enjoyed stretching their thinking to ideas that seemed to be outside of their own personal experience.

It was interesting to me and to the students to learn that almost all the characters the students developed were a composite of people they knew or had known at one time. They used their imaginations, but they also drew on their memories and experiences. We talked a lot about how everything we do and think and even imagine is influenced by who we are and what we know.

A couple of the students who did this exercise as a homework assignment, found that they got quite lost in their character. One student said that once her character had a name, the character "sort of wrote her own story – I just held the pen." Many experienced writers can only hope for such creative freedom!

Weather Moods

The weather outside can dramatically affect the mood of a classroom as well as people's desire to learn. A sunny spring day can be perfect for trying new ideas and having some fun with learning, but a cold, damp winter day can put everyone in a blue mood, making learning and teaching much more difficult.

On a particularly dreary day, the students and I talked about the effect the weather was having on our moods and our attitudes. This exercise is a result of that discussion. Once we got writing about our moods, our "blue" day brightened considerably.

Exercise Steps

1. Brainstorm "weather words". Make a list on the blackboard or have the student(s) make a list in a notebook. There are many words used to describe or explain the weather – lightning, ice, rain, tornado, wind, clouds, etc. Then have the student(s) write adjectives to go with each word – forked lightning, brittle ice, summer rain, black tornado, cold wind, fluffy clouds.
2. Discuss with the student(s) how the words used to describe weather conditions, can often be applied to our own moods or personalities – sunny disposition, thundering voice, stormy temper.
3. Ask the student(s) to use weather words to describe themselves.
4. Share your writing with one another.

Writing Examples

Fall is a change of colour and temperament for me. My personality tends to withdraw, like the summer heat. A slow lean toward total withdrawal, a show of calm before the storm. But like an Indian summer or a chinook, my affections can linger for a while before the cold starts to settle in. Sometimes my affections can be tepid and moody like fall weather that can't decide what to do, or an immediate cold front that settles in and tends to blend unnoticeably into winter.

Sheryl
Basic Job Readiness Training, Medicine Hat

[unedited freewriting] Today is another gloomy day. I sure wish this weather would smarten up. I feel it plays a big part in our lives. I don't like this rain. I feel like a yo yo, up and down and I'm sure the weather has a lot to do with it. I feel so good being in the classroom today, having Carol here is just great but I wish also that others would come. It would be so nice to see everyone. I really miss them

Sharron
Chapters, Camrose

[unedited] When I wake up in the morning I feel a little cloudy but after I get up and get moving the clouds pass and I feel clear. Sometimes when things bother me I feel like a volcano ready to explode. I never get the feeling out until I erupt and either tell someone what my problem is or I have a good cry with the feeling of rain running down my face. If I have been emotionally touched by something I feel a sensation of shivering cold but when I feel nervous or scared to do something I feel a chill that is colder than cold. When I am snuggling on the couch with my kids watching TV I feel all calm and warm.

Carol
Chapters, Camrose

Adaptations

This is a helpful exercise to build on vocabulary and practice the use of adjectives. Using weather words is an easy way to look at descriptive words and how they can be used in different ways.

When I found my students reluctant to write about themselves, I would ask them to write about their children or another family member. Sometimes it's easier to see or talk about personality traits in others rather than in ourselves.

Reflections

Weather had a surprisingly strong influence in the Chapter's classroom. For many of the students, changes in weather greatly affected their health – arthritis, migraine headaches and depression. These realities have to be taken into consideration when teaching high needs students. I tried to work with the weather so that it interfered as little as possible with our learning.

On cold days I made sure we had hot chocolate with marshmallows as a bit of a treat, and on lovely warm days we would go to the park for a picnic lunch. I made sure people had rides to class on snowy days and had the students cut cheerful pictures out of magazines as a way to start looking forward to spring. All these things helped to keep our spirits up and our focus on learning. The fact that the weather was always changing was something "I knew for sure", so it became important to work with that reality and help the students identify how they reacted to changes in the weather. They were actually surprised when they realized how much their moods and motivation could be affected by what they saw out their windows when they got up in the morning. No more climbing back into bed just because there was snow on the ground in April!

Lifetime Learning

Once the women in Chapters accepted that they were strong and capable learners, there was no stopping them. They wanted to talk about learning, to understand how we learn and why learning is so important.

One of the students commented on the questions I had asked her about school and learning during our initial interview. She said she didn't know how to answer the questions then and wanted to try answering them again. The students found the interview questions really interesting now that they were feeling stronger. They thought it would be fun to interview friends and family members to see what kind of answers other people gave. This exercise really cemented their own feelings about learning.

Exercise Steps

I have included with this chapter the set of questions the students used to do their "learning interviews". Feel free to modify the questions, use only some of them or make up your own.

1. Give your student(s) a copy of the Interview Assignment. Spend some time together talking about learning and what it means to each of you. Talk about school, successes and failures, taking risks and trying new things. Interview one another to try out the assignment questions.

2. As a homework project, ask the student(s) to find someone willing to be interviewed. (This is a good "over the weekend" assignment.) Have the students complete the interview and bring the results to class.

3. Share the interview results with one another.

   "Was it difficult to find someone willing to be interviewed? Why?"

   "What did you learn about the person you interviewed that you didn't know before?"

   Did the person you interviewed have the same ideas about learning that you do? Explain.

4. Take time to write down your feelings about learning.

5. Share your writing with one another.

Writing Examples

[unedited] I was not a learner until my eyes were opened then I realized that I have been learning all my life and the tools I used were not taught to us in school. My school was my life. I learnt my lessons threw fear and hatrid and sadness and abuce.

I learnd to be a good caring, loving person with an opend mind and open values. And if you put a book in front of me and told me to read and learn I could not do it but if you take my hand and show me I will succeed.

I am learning every day, monthe, year, minet and houre about myself and thows around me and that is the best school you could be in. I hope that people can learn the most important think in the world is that the world and people in it can teach you more than books and knowlege of facts.

Shelly
Chapters, Camrose

[unedited] Learning is the luxury and riches of the universe. Learning can allow me to be whatever - whoever - I need to be.

I always, and it seems like forever, read books. No, I devoured them with an insatiable appetite. Books were my escape. I escaped and travelled. I journied the world over and over. I could become the characters in the books. The pages became alive. I lived in the footprints of the characters. Someday I thought - someday! - the whole universe will be mine!

I marvelled at the tiniest living creature to the wonders of a double rainbow. No one, no matter what they did to me, could take away what was ingrained into my mind. It was mine forever!

Chapters is an extremely positive , reinforcing space, my space. Those who share this magical space give me hope and courage to go on. It is okay whatever I write, whatever I feel. It is okay to be on a life long journey. I can heal. I can do. I can be. I can look forward - out into the many, many wonders yet to be explored by me. Look out world, here I come!

Whitney
Chapters, Camrose

Adaptations

A lot of the questions on the Interview Assignment could lead to further writing ideas – about school, favourite teachers or why you think kids should or shouldn't stay in high school.

This might be a good time to look at learning styles – how the way we learn is very much linked to who we are as individuals.

Interviewing another person provides students with the opportunity to try out some question asking and note taking skills. Some preparation about listening skills might be helpful, too. Some of the students talked about not being taken seriously when they tried this exercise and others talked about feeling very professional being the one asking the questions. The idea for this exercise came about quite quickly so I didn't have as much time to think through the exercise as I might have. We learned a great deal after the fact, which was also valuable. It allowed for discussion about the process of learning, trial and error and learning from our experiences.

Reflections

No matter what exercise I do, or with what group, I learn something new. When I started out interviewing the first students for the Chapters Program, I asked questions that I thought were quite easy to answer. The students taught me that I was taking a lot for granted.

One of the students told me how she learned when she was little that if she broke a dish, she would get beaten. Even though she had a sense that this wasn't right, she didn't learn until she was much older that not all children were treated as she was. What she had to learn as a child was much different than what I learned as I grew up.

There are many adults in our communities who do not see themselves as people who are able to learn. They were told, often violently, that they "would never amount to anything", were "no good", or worst of all, that they were "stupid". This is one of the greatest crimes committed against the human spirit. If we do nothing else in our literacy work, we need to help those we teach to believe that they can learn, that learning is good, and that they deserve the opportunity to learn. Once a student believes that he can learn, anything is possible.

What We Are Learning
by Marie

In this program we are learning and improving one day at a time. That is a challenge in itself. We are growing as we move ahead. The program has opened new chapters to a new beginning.

We are learning new skills, not just computer and writing abilities, but the ability in ourselves to face New Challenges, to see ourselves in a positive manner. We are seeing ourselves differently, by knowing we can move on to share the creative energy within all of us.

We are giving ourselves a chance to learn a variety of writing, always open to new ideas. We are learning to be creative in all aspects of writing through short stories, poems and limericks. To take risks is to take on New Challenges.

In the program we are rediscovering ourselves. We have opened up and are exploring many ideas and doing other projects. In Chapters we are learning to become independent. We are learning that we can take the next step towards another challenge, to show others that we are in touch with our inner selves. To know we are in touch with reality gives us the chance to dream, to move towards our dreams and to reach our goals.

(*excerpted from* New Chapters)

Lifetime Learning Interview Assignment

Name: ______________________________

Age: ______________ Date: ______________________

Schooling

1. Do you remember being in Grade 1? If so, what was it like?

____

____

____

2. What did or didn't you like about school? Why?

____

____

____

3. How would a teacher describe you as a student?

____

____

____

4. Did you have a favourite teacher? What was he/she like? Did a teacher ever inspire you to do something special in your life, or to want to do something special in your life?

____

____

____

5. If you didn't finish school, was there a reason why? How old were you when you left school? Did you ever go back to school? What was that experience like?

____

____

____

Learning

6. What is something that you are good at? How did you learn to do this?

7. Can you remember a time that you learned something new and were surprised that you could do it?

8. What's the most positive learning experience you have had? Explain why it was positive.

9. In what way do you like to learn new things? By hearing them said, writing them down, reading about them, talking about them, or other ways?

10. How do you feel about taking risks/trying new things?

Response Writing

The first step to writing from the heart is to help students feel comfortable with putting their thoughts on paper. Another step is to help students feel more comfortable with their actual thoughts. Many students feel that what they have to put on paper isn't of interest or value to others, but with encouragement, support and lots of writing practice the students build the necessary confidence to explore their own thinking on paper.

Exercise Steps

1. Keep your eyes open for some good quotes that will challenge your student's thinking. They can be ideas your student(s) may agree or disagree with. Controversial statements can be great for writing and discussion.
2. Choose a quote or statement and print it out on paper so the student is able to have the words in front of him. (My students found it hard to read a blackboard and think about their responses; they wanted the words close to them so they could really see them and feel them.)
3. Have the student(s) respond to the quote.

    Do you agree with what is said?
    How does the quote make you feel?
    How do you relate to what the author says?

4. Share your writing with one another. If possible, follow up with a discussion about the quote.

    Did you all agree with the statement?
    Did different people in the group have a different interpretation?

    This is a good opportunity to talk about opinions and whether there is a right or wrong way to look at things.

Writing Examples

"Writing is hauling in a long line from the depths to find out what things are strung on it." James Moffett

[unedited] I had to read this about 5 times before I understood what it meant, but it is very true. I feel it means if we look into ourselves we will find many things we would like to write about. It could be something true that really happened or if we wanted we could let our imagination and our pen work together. When it comes to writing, the subjects to write about are never ending. I just read the quote again. I have the picture in my mind of someone fishing and every time they cast the line, they reel in a new word.

Carol
Chapters, Camrose

"Writing is a struggle against silence." Carlos Fuentes

[unedited] How can I remain silent -- when my mind is filled with a "jig saw" of bits and pieces. I feel, I hear, I see -- I ache -- I change in mid-stream as another thought "pops" into my head. My thoughts go quicker than my pen -- there is so much -- so many things just waiting to be seen -- to be explored -- to be written so others can capture the moment with me. Silence is not an efficient way of spending my time -- rarely do I feel total silence -- there's just too much activity inside -- waiting to be born -- waiting to come alive on pages. Words that encourage, words that challenge, words that heal and words that make you cry! Words to make you feel the feeling. Words to describe the beauty surrounding the darkness. Bright colours, rainbows of words -- smoky trails across the clear blue skies. Can't you see the words and the adventures in those soft billowing and fluffy white clouds? What would this world be like without words -- words that describe -- words to carry you into adventures, words to let you travel the universe. NO SILENCE FOR ME!! Words and more words -- to fill all the emptiness!

Whitney
Chapters, Camrose

"Some people want it to happen, some wish it would happen... others make it happen." author unknown

There are three different types of people: wanters, wishers and doers. Doers take the chance and go for their goal, while wanters and wishers wait, thinking that it is going to happen. We all know, deep down inside, that if we don't take the initiative, nothing will happen. I believe wanters and wishers fear failure, and this fear holds them back from trying. Doers face the fear but still tackle the challenge, seeing only the goal they will achieve at the end.

Shauna
Secretarial Refresher Program, Drumheller

Adaptations

Students can respond to anything through writing – quotes, stories, newspaper articles, children's books, or a TV program. The idea is to put responses on paper, always encouraging the students to look at how they feel about the quote or the story.

You could suggest to your student(s) that they watch a certain TV show, such as Oprah or a sitcom. Ask the student(s) to write about how they felt watching the show, then talk about it the next time you get together

Ask your students:

"Did you laugh watching the show? What made you laugh?"

"Was the show realistic? Would something like that happen in real life?"

"Were you moved by the topic? What was your opinion at the beginning of the show? What was your opinion afterward?"

Sometimes it helps to have questions prepared ahead of time as a guideline for the student(s). (When I did this, the students often asked their children to watch the show with them to help them answer the questions.)

If you are working one-on-one with a student, you might try reading a newspaper article together. The purpose of a newspaper is to inform and provide facts. Once you and your student have looked at the facts, talk (and write) about how you feel about the story. Look closely at how the facts make you feel.

We've had a good time in the classroom responding to Ann Landers' column. I give the students a person's letter to Ann then have them write advice to that person as if they were Ann. After we've heard everyone's "advice", I read Ann Lander's actual response. Many times the students disagreed with Ann and thought she hadn't considered the writer's feelings enough!

The students in Chapters are always encouraged to bring in quotes and stories that have captured their attention or imaginations. We are never without ideas and material to respond to.

Reflections

In elementary school my son kept a "response journal" where he was to respond to different stories and books the class was reading. It was hard to help him to write more than "I liked the book because the main character was a neat guy." I wanted to ask; "Why was he a neat guy? Is he anything like you? How did you feel about the things he did?" The teachers were looking for facts and comprehension; I was looking for thoughts and feelings. I know that facts are important, but that's the easy part; identifying and explaining how you feel is much harder work. It is through our feelings about the facts that we are really able to learn and understand.

Polish & Publish

Nothing gives writers more confidence than to have their words published. Unfortunately, most people think that published work has to be "saleable", ie. printed and sold. A definition from the Webster's Dictionary for the word "publish" that I particularly like is, "to put into circulation". There are many ways to have students' writings put into circulation. But first we have to talk about "polishing".

In the Chapters Program we wrote and wrote and wrote, without worrying about punctuation or spelling or grammar. We wrote to get our thoughts on paper. But when the time came to show our work to the outside world, we took our pieces of writing and thoughtfully began the process of polishing our work.

> *"First you find the gold, then you go back and polish it."*
>
> *Joel Saltzman,*
> *If You Can Talk You Can Write*

To polish means to rethink, revise and rewrite each line and each paragraph of writing. Well-known writers say that they rewrite everything they write at least five times before it is published.

> *"I have never thought of as myself as a good writer. Anyone who wants reassurance of that should read one of my first drafts. But I'm one of the best rewriters."*
>
> *James A. Mitchener*

When we are doing day-to-day writing exercises, I suggest that the students put a star on the top of the pages of writing they like or are pleased with. (When someone reads a piece of writing out loud that gives the others the GBTs, right away someone says, "Better put a star on that one!") That way the students have a number of pieces to work with when we decide to do some polishing.

The students really look forward to polishing their writing, especially the pieces they are proud of. They have learned that "the red pen" provides them with ideas to improve their work. Before, they had only seen "corrections" as criticism, not suggestions for improvement. The first time we go through the process of editing their work in preparation for publication, the students are quite uncomfortable and unsure of themselves. Once they see their stories in print, however, they are ecstatic. They soon learn to trust the process.

We have "put into circulation" or published our work in the local newspaper, literacy journals and newsletters, research reports, brochures, posters and self-published booklets. Some of the students have had their work published in church bulletins, national magazines and anthologies. Even though they haven't been paid for their work, the students enjoy calling themselves "published writers". And so they should. The process of preparing work for publication is an act of determination, discipline and faith.

Exercise Steps

1. Ask your student(s) to go back through their binders or notebooks and find a piece of writing that appeals to them.
2. Have them read their work and see how they feel about it now. Aside from spelling and punctuation, what improvements would they like to make?
3. If you are in a classroom, have the student(s) read their piece out loud for feedback from the other students. If you are working one-to-one, you can still answer these questions with your student.

    "What did you like about this piece of writing?"

    "Is there information missing?"

    "Does the writer get her point across?"

    "Do you have any ideas on how the writing could be improved?"

4. Now, as the instructor, read the student's story and offer your suggestions, including spelling, sentence structure, punctuation.
5. As an assignment, ask the student(s) to polish a piece of writing well enough to read it out loud. (Some of the students who were particularly shy or uncomfortable with their reading ability asked me to read their stories for them.)

Writing Examples

Unedited

herоs come in difrent shapes an sises. Som are tall or samll, some ar hppe or glad. But the 1 hero I see coms out from within you and me. IT is that part of us that shos the werld that we care. If you are doun it will froun for awhile then your hero will say I am stil here don't be so hard on yerself.

She is my frend and my pal and my budy. That person who knos me beter than i kno myself. she is the valus of who you are. Som call her ther consiense, som call her ther hart. But to me she is the valus that my mom tot to me she is who Shelly really is.

Edited

Hero

Heroes come in different shapes and sizes. Some are tall or small, some are happy or glad. But one hero I see comes out from within you and me. It is that part of us that shows the world that we care. If you are down, she will frown for awhile, then your hero will say, "I am here. Don't be so hard on yourself".

She is my friend, my pal and my buddy. She is the person who knows me better than I know myself. She is the values of who I am. Some call her their conscience, some call her their heart. But to me, she is the values that my mom taught to me. She is who Shelly really is.

Shelly
Chapters, Camrose

Adaptations

The definition of publishing being "put into circulation" works well with the idea of reading work out loud. To get used to the idea of having an audience (ie. the fact that others would be hearing or reading our words) we had a formal "reading" in the classroom. Everyone had at least one piece to read. The students each stood up in front of the class and read the polished version of their thoughts and stories. They told each other why they chose this piece and how they felt about reading it.

There is certainly a physical and emotional transition for students to be able (like all writers) to let go of their words, to put them into circulation. Take time to talk about this "letting go". It is one thing to take the risk to put your words on paper, but another to have others read or hear the words. The students had a lot of questions and concerns at first:

> "What if my family doesn't like what I said?"
> "What if people think what I wrote sounds too much like Grade 5 writing?"
> "How do I know people won't laugh at me?"

We had to take a lot of time to work through our feelings about being "in the limelight". Some of the students decided to use a pen name, some credited their pieces with only their first names. They were given the freedom to deal with their concerns in the way that worked best for them. Most of the students were very private people, some literally for reasons of personal safety. Even with their doubts, the students were proud of what they had written. Needless to say, our first publication was an overwhelming success and not one student received a negative comment about their work.

Reflections

Polishing writing is simply part of the writing process. Once the students understood that, they were eager to polish more of their work. With all the freewriting and writing exercises we did, it wasn't long before they had pages and pages of writing in their binders – obvious proof that they could write.

Putting together a publication can be long and tedious work, and as with most publishing projects, we ended up working to deadlines. All the teamwork skills and strengths the group had developed over the weeks of writing together sure came through while we were in production.

To celebrate our work and our writing, we held a "book launch" for our first booklet publication. We invited friends and family, local dignitaries and the press. We had snacks and coffee and even an autographing table (all designed and prepared by the students). One of my friends who works at the TD Bank took her new copy of *The Hearts of Women* back to the bank with her, then half an hour later called to ask for 20 more copies; all the women there wanted their own copy! These were professional working women who had been moved by what the students had written. That phone call was a true moment of success for the students. All the hours of rewriting and rethinking and rewriting again, had paid off. They were no longer afraid of their audience.

Feeling Good

I have never met anyone who said they were sorry they had taken the time to write something down. Nor have I met anyone who said they wished they had never learned to write. Writing is not something we regret doing; it is something that brings us pleasure, insight and release. It feels good.

Before I came to the Chapters Program I never took much time to write. Except maybe an occasional letter or grocery list. I never was very good at writing essays in high school. I never could focus my thoughts about the subject the essays were to be on. Therefore I always had poor marks on them. In school there was so much put on perfection for essays or anything we had to write about. In Chapters we aren't pushed to perfection. Anything we write is OK.

With heart writing we're not worried about perfection. We don't have to be afraid of getting criticised about what we wrote. Everything is fine. I like that. No pressures to be perfectionists. Everything we write is good! This program has made writing from the heart, writing out loud what it's all about. I feel good about the writing we do here.

To write daily in a gratitude journal has given me a purpose to sit down and write. Something I never thought much of before. Now it seems I can't get enough of it. I tend to write novels - pages and pages of stuff. There's no end to what I need to write it seems. I've even tried to write poems. Sometimes they seem they hardly make sense to me, but I try.

Writing has built my self-esteem up, in everything I do. By sharing stories, poems and freewriting in class, I've learned to laugh again. That's what writing has done for me. It has built up my confidence to laugh again.

We are not all the same even when it comes to writing. Each of us has our own unique ways of expression. But it feels good because it comes from within, from the heart.

Alice
Chapters, Camrose

The Love of Writing

Freewriting January 25, 1995

[unedited] I am very glad to be back here at Chapters. I didn't fully realize how much I had missed this place until I reentered this morning. One thing that I am getting out of this course is a desire to write. I found this weekend my hand was actually itching to write!! Maybe I'll catch up on all my correspondence now. I still have forgotten to bring a picture of Matthew to show everyone here. My thoughts are kind of muddled right now, a lot of disjointed thoughts running through my mind but I'm glad to be writing right now.

April
Chapters, Camrose

Freewriting January 15, 1997

[unedited] I find writing relaxes me. I can put my jumbled feelings down on paper, taking the pressure off my brain. It makes for a healthier me. I sometimes get to sentimental to say things I want to say and by writing I can say them on paper. I also like writing because of my poems. I can relate to my life's experiences, it's like a diary for me to look back on. Also I hope one day to become a famous poet.

Sharron
Chapters, Camrose

April and Sharron are not the only ones who expressed a new-found pleasure in writing. Marg Reine, a handbook field tester in Edmonton, sent me these thoughts, written by one of the students she had been working with at the Prospects Literacy Program.

(I like to write)... because it's something different and challenging. Also I learned to express myself on paper. At least I can write a sentence now, even if it's a short one. My spelling is improving very noticeably. I do notice this and I'm learning to "pat myself on the back". I am more confident now.

Just today, I filled out an application without any help. This is a first! "Practice makes perfect". So now I'm more confident about my ability to write because I've been practising.

In Wetaskiwin, Veronica Park has been field-testing exercises with her ESL class. This is what they have to say about writing:

You learn English through writing and that helps to develop your confidence.

The more we practise, the easier it is to get our ideas on paper.

Writing helps you think, helps to sort out ideas.

Its hard not to worry about spelling and getting it right.

Writing helps you improve your level of English.

Pat Anderson, a field tester and life skills coach, asked her students in the New Worlds for Women Program in Drumheller why they like to write. These are some of the students' responses:

Writing helps me sort out my thoughts.

I enjoy writing as it helps me know what I need to say.

I find it soothing and it keeps my thoughts together.

I like to write as it helps me to sort out what I'm thinking. Also I like to be able to look back on it.

I like to write because it helps me get my feelings out and it clears my mind.

I like to write to express my feelings and thoughts in a way that sometimes can't be said.

I like to write because writing is the only way I can get all my feelings out and it doesn't have to hurt anybody.

Of course, not all the responses to a question like "Why do you like to write?" will be positive. At least not at first. One of Pat's students wrote:

I don't particularly like to write. My thoughts are too scrambled and I don't like the way they end up on paper. I have problems writing personal thoughts and feelings on paper. I don't like them out where people can read them.

Many of my students felt exactly the same way about writing. But that reluctance and fear changed with time, practice and a lot of encouragement. After attending a writing workshop I taught for students in a Basic Job Readiness Program in Medicine Hat, one student wrote:

I was nervous at first, but you did help me feel comfortable. I did enjoy the writing exercises and I think I will continue to practice. This is a hard time in my life right now every new step is intimidating but the class was comfortable. I look forward to more of this type of writing exercise.

The following piece of freewriting of Barb's from Chapters is one of my favourites because it shows so well how often our students think they can't write, when in fact they are wonderful writers.

I love writing. Other people's writing, that is. I think it is so exciting, adventurous and brave to transform your thoughts on to paper. I am talking about writing from the heart writing. I am having trouble getting my own thoughts on paper as I think I have to say something like it has never been said before otherwise it is not good enough and this all of course, is a delusion or distorted thinking of self pity, self absorption or should I say my obsession with myself. There, it is coming now.

I am so convinced that writing is a healthy academic and intellectual pursuit, that I continue to encourage my students to write, to get past their fears and frustrations about writing, to get to the point where writing feels good. Here are some more thoughts about writing from the students in Pat Anderson's class:

Writing slows down my pace. I have found that it relaxes me and gives me an overall peaceful feeling.

It lets me feel free to grow and strengthens my ability to feel the need to grow. I have grown a lot (through my writing). Now when it comes to freewriting, I can usually think of something to write, either my children or something that has happened last night or yesterday. I love to write about my children, the funny things they say and do.

I've become more in touch with my inner feelings and thoughts because of doing writing.

I've gotten to know myself better.

I have grown by my writing in many ways. I thought that I could never write, now I love it.

Writing has taught me that putting things on paper is a good way of letting feelings out.

I have found writing to be almost therapy. I really love it. It has taught me to express myself more. I never knew how much I'd enjoy it.

Take a Bow

In all honestly, I didn't have any idea how much the students I worked with would come to love writing, or how much they would be able to grow and learn through their writing. We were all so excited about what was happening in the Chapters classroom when we first started that we decided to do some conference presentations about Chapters.

In 1994, Carol, Whitney, Sheilah and Shelly made a presentation at the AAAL Conference in Slave Lake. None of the students had ever spoken in front of an audience before. When asked on the session evaluation forms what they liked most, people attending the workshop wrote:

> *I liked the sharing of stories of the participants and the growth they have experienced in the process.*
>
> *These people are honestly a team. No wonder you're all pulling ahead.*
>
> *The students from Chapters are real, have overcome great difficulties, have terrific self-esteem and yet have such a humble, warm, intimate approach.*
>
> *Writing obviously really helps people get out of their shells. The students from Chapters were very inspiring. It made me feel very good.*
>
> *I am encouraged to involve as many of our students in a similar fashion. I hope I won't be too impatient!*

A letter I received after that Conference from Jocelyn Doucet, a literacy coordinator in Fahler, Alberta made all the student's hours of nervous hard work well worth it:

> *After attending your Chapters session, I felt that your evaluation form was not sufficient.*
>
> *First of all, I understand now what you meant by GBTs. I felt them. There was a magic that was happening and I was only there for 1 1/2 hours.*

It did my heart good to know that it is possible for such tremendous healing to take place. And I want the group to know that I believe that it is people like Shelly, Sheilah, Whitney and Carol who will save us and not scientists or lawmakers.

Chapters gave me hope and opened up a world of possibilities. The words 'Thank you' just don't seem enough. But I do thank you for sharing so much so unselfishly.

This is my evaluation and I am saying, YES, I liked everything about the session, and YES it was valuable beyond measure. Rating - 10/10!

The next year, Shelly, Sharron and Sue made a presentation at the AAAL Conference in Calgary. By this time, we were really ready to talk more about writing and how we used students' everyday experiences as the curriculum for the program. People who attended the session said:

I enjoyed the students talking about their personal experiences with writing. I was really impressed.

It was very satisfying to take the discussion from the intellectual level to the feeling level.

I liked the writing that came from the heart, the risk taking.

I liked the fact that students took part. It showed how well safety works.

It was great to have students sharing their stories. It's heartening to see programs that still have the freedom to allow for personal discovery and growth while learning.

The students in Chapters have inspired me to start writing for myself more. I do lots of writing at work and sometimes it even has a voice, although much of it is pretty sterile. Your workshop told me that while I may not always need writing for deep therapy, I could often use it for simple pleasure.

And in 1996, Sharron, Alice and Barb made a presentation at the AAAL Conference in Vermilion. Fifty people attended the Chapters session. The students had taken some of their favourite exercises from the field testing draft of *Writing Out Loud* to try with the session participants. The participants were asked to do some writing and read their writing out loud. The audience was a wonderful mix of government representatives, students, administrators and instructors. This is what they said about the session:

Pressure sometimes brings out real gems of thought.

Well, I've always loved to write, but I learned today that I don't need to fear sharing my thoughts.

I found out today that I am capable of writing something that gave someone else the GBTs!

I can see that I am out of touch with writing and must get back to it again.

I have always loved writing, but I didn't know how easy it was to get others going.

I can write better than I thought I could!

My journal entry for February 28, 1997

Most of the students who came to the Chapters Program were discouraged with life. They were tired, bruised, scared and ready to give up. I have watched 30 women over the past 3 years gain confidence, laugh again, rediscover themselves as learners and build a new relationship with life and the world around them. I watched them wrestle with their thoughts and feelings as they put them on paper, and watched them smile when they read something out loud to others in the group that made sense and felt right. I still marvel at the fact that I was lucky enough to be part of all that.

After a workshop I taught at the University of Alberta for students working on a Masters of Adult Education, Natalia Toroshenko, also a literacy coordinator with Lakeland College wrote:

"Thank you Deb, for sharing with us a piece of the world that is turning as things should. Too often I get caught up in the frustration and struggle of daily realities (ugly as they sometimes are) and forget that hope and a positive outlook are necessary to keep moving forward without too many steps back."

I know that having a positive outlook works. And I know that writing works. I remember feeling really sure of that when one of the Chapters students returned from the U of A Hospital in Edmonton with a handful of pages she had written while she sat in a doctor's waiting room. She couldn't find any paper, so ended up writing six pages of thoughts and fears on the back of hospital maps that were on the table in the waiting room! Rosemarie laughed as she told us how she "just needed to write" and how she did whatever she had to to find some paper to write on.

I am so grateful that being part of the Chapters program meant that I also had the opportunity to write. Three years ago I only had a vague idea about what it meant to write from the heart. And now I can't imagine my life without time to write every day. The brave spirited students I worked with are not the only ones to have found a voice. I, too, have discovered that I have pages to write and so much to say. I love writing out loud. I love the way it feels to scribble down the words and the way I feel when I put down my pen and sit back and look at the words on the page. Magic? (There's that word again.) Who knows.

Maybe I don't need to question it anymore, the magic I mean. So many people have told me that writing has come to mean more to them than they ever thought it would or could. They have found their own reasons for writing, their own magic, and that's all that matters.

Thank You To Chapters

by Sharron

When we feel we've reached an end
To learning what we want
Someone will take our place
Through Chapters we'll move on.

I'm looking forward to the time
When I'll look back and say
"Look what Chapters did for me
I really am OK."

The work I've done throughout the years
Has brought me joy and pride
A little pain along the way
That I so easily hide.

I'm ready now to face the world
And show what I can do
I have a bit of part time work
And hope it sees me through.

I've met so many people now
That are so nice to me
I realize in Chapters
They really care you see.

I'm going to the future now
That I have found for me
Chapters played a part in it
And I thank you graciously.

Bibliography

Books and more books! I had almost no resources when I started the Chapters Program. Now I have a bookshelf full of books I treasure. As the program grew and evolved, I wanted to know everything I could about writing and tapping into our creativity and about personal growth and self-discovery. This bibliography is the best of what I found through frequenting new and used book stores, ordering from catalogues, snooping through my friends' libraries and listening to the recommendations of my colleagues. In this bibliography, you will find a list of:

Books that encourage writing
Books to help free our creativity
Books about life skills
Books especially for women
More books with good ideas
Reports about the Chapters Program

If you have some other favourites, I'd love to hear about them. Some of the students contributed book titles and let me know which of the books I used in the classroom had helped them. You will notice that some of the book annotations are prefaced with "reviewed by" Sharron, Alice or Barb, three students from the Chapters Program. They offered to help with the bibliography; their honest and heartfelt book reviews are a pleasure to read.

I also included the name of the reports that were submitted to our funders over the years. All our research and the thought behind the development of the Chapters Program is documented in these reports.

I hope you are able to find some inspiration in these books. These are not books about grammar and spelling or teaching business English. These are books about getting to the heart of writing and getting to know ourselves as creative human beings. Happy reading!

Books that Encourage Writing

Barasovska, Joan (1978) *I Wish I Could Write*, New York: New Reader's Press

When I first started out as a tutor, this little book was my favourite "idea book". I thought it was out of print, but was happy to learn that it is still available through Artel Educational Resources, Burnaby, B.C. (1-800-665-9255) for $6.95.

Bennett, Hal Zina (1995) *Writing From the Heart*, Mill Valley, CA: Nataraj Publishing

From the jacket cover: "Bennett practices writing as a spiritual path. He teaches with the compassion and wisdom born of experience and humility. Writers, and those who wish to be, are well served by his insight , candour and humour – one of the handful of real writing books." Julia Cameron, author of *The Artist's Way*

Brande, Dorthea (1934) *Becoming a Writer*, New York: G.P. Putnam's Sons

I found this to be a fascinating book. Brande taught writing courses in the 1930s and believes very much what I do. She says, "I think there is a magic and that it is teachable. This book is about the writer's magic." In *Becoming a Writer*, Brande has a sound, practical, inspirational and down to earth approach to writing and the personality of the writer that is both familiar and refreshing.

Burnham, Sophy (1994) *For Writers Only*, New York, Ballantine Books

This book doesn't give advice on the techniques of writing, but rather talks about the emotions great writers go through – from the exquisite pain to heady joy – in the process of putting words on paper and having their work published.

Capacchione, Lucia (1979) *The Creative Journal: The Art of Finding Yourself*, California: New Castle Publishing Co., Inc.

(reviewed by Sharron) I hadn't thought before about drawing in a journal. I thought a journal had to be writing. But drawing is a way of expressing your inner thoughts too. It's a great idea! I sure found out that there are still a lot of things "out there" that I have yet to explore.

I think it would be a good idea for an instructor to ask the student to journal creatively for a week and then share the journal with each other. It would be different for some people, but it's still a really good way to get your feelings out, especially for people who don't think they're very good at writing.

Dodd, Anne Wescott (1973) *Write Now! Insights Into Creative Writing*, New York: Global Book Company, Inc.

This book was a garage sale find – a discard from a high school cooperative program. Even though it's 25 years old and geared to high school age, it's still a terrific resource, full of free thinking and creative ideas from the '70's. Most of the exercises encourage writing about social issues from racism to poverty to staying in school.

Elbow, Peter (1981) *Writing With Power: Techniques for Mastering the Writing Process*, New York: Oxford University Press

The author says, "Writing with power doesn't just mean getting power over readers. It means getting power over yourself and over the writing process: knowing what you are doing as you write, figuring out what you really mean; being in charge, having control; not feeling stuck or helpless or intimidated." Good reading for anyone who wants to do more writing.

Goldberg, Bonnie (1996) *Room to Write*, New York: G.P. Putnam's Sons

(reviewed by Alice) I liked this book because it's full of fun, creative ways to write. And what to write. You can start from nothing and write great stories or just phrases from the top of your head.

The book talked about doubting your ability to write. That is the way I feel, especially if I try to write poetry. I criticize my writing and myself a lot. In this book, self-doubt soon becomes "I can do it! I can write!" It seems like the more I write, the more I want to write. My need to write becomes an obsession to make sure it's the one thing I do everyday, even if it's just a little writing. This book makes me feel excited about writing.

Goldberg, Natalie (1986) *Writing Down the Bones – Freeing the Writer Within*, New York: Random House, Inc.

Ms. Goldberg tells wonderful stories about writing – both as a teacher and as a writer herself. I love this book. I keep it by my bed and read it often. I'm always guaranteed to come across a new idea for an exercise or an insight that encourages me to keep writing.

__________ (1990) *Wild Mind: Living The Writer's Life*, New York: Bantam Books

As someone hoping to spend more and more time writing, I found this honest account of a writer's life insightful, intriguing and irresistible.

Hagberg, Janet O. (1995) *Wrestling With Your Angels: A Spiritual Journey to Great Writing*, Massachusetts, Adams Publishing

The author believes that we write with two companions on our shoulders: the critic on one side (who wants to destroy our confidence) and an angel on the other (who helps us reach into our souls to produce great writing). This book is full of exercises to help us develop "writing with soul".

Kazemek, Francis E. & Pat Rigg (1995) *Enriching Our Lives: Poetry Lessons for Adult Literacy Teachers and Tutors*, Delaware: International Reading Association

This is an easy-to-use, hands-on book that will have you writing poetry before you know it. I'm not a poet, but I spent an evening with *Enriching Our Lives* and had a wonderful time trying Haiku and Grocery List Poems. Kazemek and Rigg are as enthusiastic about poetry as I am about writing from the heart. They believe that "poetry helps us understand ourselves and our worlds; it helps us see ourselves and our world in new ways".

Keyes, Ralph (1995) *The Courage to Write: How Writers Transcend Fear*, New York: Henry Holt & Company

It takes courage to put words on paper. My students often talked about the fear of others reading their words, the fear of being criticised, and the fear of feeling vulnerable. This book really helped me understand how fear affects our ability to write (and write well) and what steps we can take to get past the fear. I also found some great quotes in this book to prove to my students that ALL writers experience feelings of fear.

Klauser, Henriette Anne (1995) *Put Your Heart On Paper: Staying Connected In a Loose Ends World*, New York: Bantam Books

(reviewed by Alice) I would greatly recommend this book because there is a lot of heart writing and ideas on how to get people to communicate to each other. Like letter writing only more often. It doesn't have to be long letters, just a few lines to get things going. We can learn a lot through heart writing. When we do writing from the heart in Chapters, we learn about each other and we get closer. I like to write short notes to my kids because in this world there are a lot of things that pull families apart. You can live in the same house and not have much communication, so heart writing to each other is good!

__________ (1987) *Writing on Both Sides of the Brain: Breakthrough Techniques for People Who Write,* New York: Harper Collins Publishers

We use the left side of our brain when we want to be logical, analytical and rational. We use the right side of our brain when we want to be intuitive or romantic. Klauser argues that even though the left and right sides of our brain have different thinking functions, we are most effective in our writing when we use our whole brain. This book provides the writer with exercises to tap into and utilize our different ways of thinking.

Mueller, Lavonne & Jerry D. Reynolds, (1982) *Creative Writing,* Toronto: Doubleday Canada Ltd.

This is an easy-to-read, well-designed book with sections on writing stories, poetry and one-act plays. There is also a helpful section on "Making It Public"; the publishing and promotion of writing.

Rainer, Tristine (1978) *The New Diary,* New York: St. Martin's Press

I was given this book years ago when I first started doing personal writing to document my learning. It is still one of the best books available on how to use a journal for self-discovery and creativity.

Rico, Gabriele Lusser (1983) *Writing the Natural Way: Using Right Brain Techniques to Release Your Expressive Powers,* New York: G.P. Putnam's Sons

Rico believes that "writing is a much more natural process if we learn to flow with, rather than fight, the natural cooperative rhythms of the hemispheres of our brain." This book offers the idea of "clustering" words and ideas as a "brainstorming process what will put you in touch with the subject matter of your writing".

__________ (1991) *Pain and Possibility: Writing Your Way Through Personal Crisis,* New York: G.P. Putnam's Sons

I am fascinated by Rico's use of "clustering – a non linear writing process" to heal emotional pain and transform it into new possibilities for personal growth. This is however, a fairly in-depth study and requires attentive reading to understand the concepts presented in the book.

Ruc, Rebecca & Susan Wheeler (1993) *Creating The Story: Guides for Writers*, New Hampshire: Heinemann Educational Books, Inc.

This is a book about writing stories – with easy-to-read guidelines and ideas about plot, characters and point of view, and a particularly good section on revising, editing and publishing your work.

Saltzman, Joel (1993) *If You Can Talk You Can Write,* New York: Warner Books

(reviewed by Barb) This book spoke of my problem right away, in short, understandable statements. It would be great if I could write down some of the things I say as I ramble on about them. I usually start out to write with definite criteria that it better sound good and make sense so I usually defeat myself before I get started.

I love what the book says about the "Killer P's – Perfectionism, Paralysis and Procrastination". I think that names the problem for a lot of people. In knowing the problems, we can start dealing with them and start writing with a new positive outlook.

Most people can't determine what it is about writing that deters them. This book identifies the problem and offers insightful and funny solutions. It's funny and heartwarming. It is not dry stuff. It is enlightening and frees you up and makes you feel lighter.

Sanek, Willett (1996) *Writing Your Life: Putting Your Past on Paper,* New York: Avon Books

Sanek believes that we all have stories to tell, and that our stories are wonderful substance for creative non fiction writing. He says, "Writing from memory allows you to time-travel, to zoom back to people and places you have not seen in years. Buckle your seat belt. This trip could be the exhilarating escapade you've been itching for." He offers some good ideas for tapping into the best of our childhood memories.

Woodrow, Helen (and contributors) (1994) *From the Shoreline, Writing Instruction in Adult Literacy and Basic Education* Available from Educational Planning and Design Associates, 18 Leslie Street, St. John's Newfoundland A1E 2V6 (709) 753-8815

There is very little instructional material available that is specifically addresses teaching writing to literacy students. It has been a great pleasure to read and learn from this truly Canadian resource.

Woodrow, Helen & Mary Norton (1996) *Propriety and Possibilities*, Newfoundland: Harish Press

Following the success of *A Newfoundland Spell*, a collection of writing by basic education students in Newfoundland, Woodrow and Norton wrote *Propriety and Possibility* as a companion book to describe the activities and strategies used to encourage and support writing development with adults. It also includes a critical discussion about instructional practices. Copies of both publications are available from The Learning Centre, 10116 – 105 Avenue, Edmonton, T5H 0S2.

Zinsser, William (1994) *On Writing Well*, New York: HarperCollins Publishers

This book is probably the most technical book you will find in this bibliography (good information on style, audience, writing about people, etc.) but I've included it because it is written in such a strong, well-organized, personable and informal manor that it is easy reading. An author, editor and teacher, Zinsser tells his students that "You have to be able to write a succession of clear, decent sentences, but that's not to say that you can't write in your own voice." He also says: "Writing isn't a skill that some people are born with and others aren't, like art or music. Writing is thinking on paper, or talking to someone on paper. If you can think clearly, or if you can talk to someone about the things you know and care about, you can write – with confidence and enjoyment."

Books that Help Free Our Creativity

Cameron, Julia (1992) *The Artist's Way*, New York: G.P. Putnam's Sons

__________ (1996) *The Vein of Gold*, New York: G.P. Putnam's Sons

Both of Cameron's books are books that nudge the reader closer to her creative centre. Both books offer a strict program to follow to help "recover our creativity" which Cameron believes has been "buried alive under a mountain of negative conditioning". Anyone serious about wanting to get better acquainted with their inner selves, to opening themselves up to greater creativity, will love these books. Start with *The Artist's Way* . The program in *The Vein of Gold* requires an even greater commitment.

Cook, Marshall J. (1992) *Freeing Your Creativity: A Writer's Guide*, Ohio: F&W Publishers, inc.

From the jacket cover: "Marshall Cook teaches you how to banish the fears, bad habits and excuses that have sent your muse into hiding. You'll learn to link your rationality with your creativity to increase your productivity. And you'll discover you can be passionate in all areas of your writing, including steps like research and editing."

Ealy, C. Diane (1995) *The Woman's Book of Creativity*, Hillsboro, Oregon: Beyond Words Publishing, Inc.

Women are naturally creative, but as women, we tend to limit our creativity to how to make our kid's lunches something nutritious that they'll still eat. This book is not about writing – it's about giving ourselves permission and encouragement to be creative in our thinking, in all areas of our life.

Jeffers, Susan (1987) *Feel the Fear and Do It Anyway,* New York: Random House, Inc.

I included this book in the bibliography because I have found fear to be one of the biggest stumbling blocks our students face (and of course, as instructors, we have our own share of fears). Fear stops us from trying, from hoping, from thinking past today. Jeffer's book offers a direct and honest (and often humourous) approach to meeting our fears head on.

Marsel, Eric (1995) *Fearless Creating*, New York: G.P. Putnam's Sons

I have read this book from cover to cover – twice. I love the way it's presented, what it has to say, and how it makes me feel when I read it. This book is for anyone who wants to understand more about the creative process. Wonderful exercises and good, solid instruction and direction.

Sark (1992) *Inspiration Sandwich: Stories to Inspire Our Creative Freedom*, California: Celestial Arts

(reviewed by Barb) This book is mystical, magical, awe-inspiring, innocent and hopeful. In reading this book, I learned that to be innocent and fun-loving and silly is very important and that it's okay to love that side of myself. Silly thoughts can be profound when they're put down on paper with ink.

This book teaches you to explore yourself and life with sensitivity and fun. Anything and everything is possible. I like the idea of free hand, free spirit. This book is inspiring totally – I could really just eat it up!

__________ (1994) *Living Juicy: Creative morsels for your creative soul*, California: Celestial Arts

(reviewed by Sharron) This book immediately caught my eye because it's so colourful. When I read the title 'Living Juicy' I just had to dive in and find out just what this was all about.

I learned so much about myself in this book. It gives so many fun examples about life that I think it would be fun to try some of the ideas in the classroom. I think we could come up with some juicy, gooey answers and discussions.

It tells everything in such an open, simple manner. It sums up pretty well everything we want to know about ourselves – our thoughts, our feelings, our frustrations and ways to deal with them. And much, much more.

Simmons, Susan Lepage (1994) *What If? 310 Bite Size Brain Snacks to Spark Your Creative Spirit*, Canada: I.C. Creative! The Simmons Group

There are lots of thought-provoking ideas to spark your imagination. "What if you gave yourself an entire play day to do anything you wanted?" or "What if you could drive a flying saucer from midnight until six o'clock in the morning?" There is no end to the pages of ideas these questions could have you writing about!

Stoddard, Alexandra (1986) *Living a Beautiful Life: 500 Ways to Add Elegance, Order, Beauty and Joy to Every Day of Your Life*, New York: Avon Books

__________ (1995) *The Art of the Possible – The path from perfectionism to balance and freedom*, New York: William Morrow and Company, Inc.

Both of Stoddard's books have been a helpful resource for me in helping my students find ways to make what seems ordinary into the extraordinary, to make the best out of what is already available. The ideas in these books follows the thinking that "Anything is possible".

Books About Life Skills

(Please note that all the resources provided in the Life Skills section of this Bibliography were recommended by Glenda Staples, Life Skills Instructor at Medicine Hat College. If you would like more information about Life Skills resources, instruction or becoming a Life Skills Coach, Glenda can be reached at (403) 529-3957.)

Allen, Shirley; Mickey Mehal, Sally Patmateer and Ron Sluser (1995) *The New Dynamics of Life Skills Coaching*, YWCA of Metropolitan Toronto*

This manual is an absolute must for anyone interested in gaining more understanding of Life Skills. Included in the manual is information of Life Skills definition, philosophy and theory. Combined with this is some very practical information regarding group dynamics and behaviours. This would be of particular interest to anyone who is working with groups on an ongoing basis and has experienced some of the issues that can arise in a group.

Discovering Life Skills Volume 1 – 5, YWCA of Metropolitan Toronto*

These Life Skills manuals contain complete lesson plans on all areas of Life Skills. There are lessons on self-awareness, communication skills, building relationships, problem-solving, fitness and leisure, employment and community resources. Each lesson has exercises, activities and theory related to the topic. Some of the lessons include writing activities, and many of those that don't could be adapted to include more writing.

YWCA Communicating Assertively Manual for Group Facilitators (1991) YWCA of Metropolitan Toronto*

Although this manual deals primarily with communication skills, it also includes some ideas on building self-esteem and utilizing the problem-solving methodology. There is a video that can be ordered with the manual. This video deals almost exclusively with assertiveness and being able to identify the differences between assertive, aggressive and non assertive behaviour. This material would be appropriate for anyone teaching assertiveness, but otherwise is not a necessary resource.

Discovering Life Skills Teaching Employment Groups Volume VII (1995) YWCA of Metropolitan Toronto*

Another excellent manual from the Toronto YWCA. As well as dealing with employment specific skills, this manual also includes information on self-esteem, problem-solving, change, goal-setting, stress management and communicating effectively. Again, many of the exercises in this manual could be adapted to writing exercises. A "must have" for anyone working with groups that have an end goal of employment.

**Copies of the preceding books published by the YWCA of Metropolitan Toronto can be purchased by contacting:*

YWCA of Metropolitan Toronto

phone (416) 961-8100
fax (416) 961-7739

Publications Department
80 Woodlawn Avenue E
Toronto ON
M4T 1C1

Canfield, Jack & Frank Siccone (1995) *101 Ways to Develop Student Self-esteem and Responsibility*, Massachusetts: Allyn and Bacon

Although this book is written for teachers working with children, most of the exercises and concepts are transferable to the adult learner. I have used a number of the exercises with adults and have had great success with them. There are actually 101 activities described in the book, many of which are writing exercises. An excellent resource book for building self-esteem and responsibility.

Branden, Nathaniel (1983) *The Art of Self-Discovery*, New York: Bantam Books

__________ (1983) *Honouring the Self: Self-Esteem and Personal Transformation*, New York: Bantam Books

Nathaniel Branden is considered to be one of the leading authorities on self-esteem. In these two books he looks at the issues surrounding self-esteem and provides techniques for increasing it. The author advocates the power of sentence completion in becoming more aware of the self. Both books provide a variety of sentence stems to use in becoming more self-aware. While all of Branden's books contain excellent information, the writing exercises that he uses are ones that are done in a therapeutic setting, and caution needs to be exercised in using them in a classroom setting.

__________ (1994) *Six Pillars of Self-Esteem*, New York: Bantam Books

This resource provides information on self-esteem, how it affects our lives and how to build it. Also included in Branden's work are some completion exercises to develop internal sources of self-esteem.

Dyer, Wayne W. (1989) *You'll See It When You Believe It*, New York: William Morrow and Company, inc.

As with most of Dyer's books, this is another excellent resource of self-actualization. This book deals with the importance of being able to first visualize our goals, and then have that visualization manifest itself in our lives.

Books Especially for Women

Albert, Susan Wittig (1996) *Writing From Life – A Journey of Self-Discovery for Women*, New York: G.P. Putnam's Sons

Wittig is an author and writing instructor who believes in the power of telling and recording our stories. Designed especially for women, *Writing From Life* provides the reader with writing exercises, meditations and samples of women's writing to move the telling of our stories to the written word. "*Writing from Life* will convince you that every woman's life is worth writing."

Ban Breathnach, Sarah (1995) *Simple Abundance: A Daybook of Comfort & Joy*, New York: Warner Books Inc.

Every woman should own a copy of *Simple Abundance*. It truly is a book that brings comfort and joy. Spending time with this book has had a profound and positive effect on the the direction of my life and the life of many of my students.

Louden, Jennifer (1992) *The Woman's Comfort Book: A Self-Nurturing Guide to Restoring Balance to your Life*, New York: Harper Collins Publishers

This book is full of warm and engaging ideas to help women nurture their bodies, minds and spirits. It gives us encouragement and permission to treat ourselves with the love and care we deserve.

Making Connections – Literacy and EAL Curriculum from a Feminist Perspective (1996) Canadian Congress for Learning Opportunities for Women. Copies available from CCLOW, 47 Main Street, Toronto, Ontario M4E 2V6 (416) 699-1909

I wish this resource had been available years ago! It is a book full of literacy and life skills activities, readings and lesson plans specific to women and women's issues. The book also comes with a cassette tape with songs that are referred to in two chapters of the book. *Making Connections* is an invaluable resource for anyone working with women's groups.

Schiwy, Marlene A. (1996) *A Voice of Her Own: Women and the Journal-Writing Journey*, New York: Fireside

(reviewed by Sharron) I had a good feeling when I read the title of the book. I hadn't thought about journal-writing as a journey before. It really made me want to read what was inside and as I read it, I understood more about what keeps me writing in my journal. My journal has given me a place to sort out my thoughts and I know that I write more about my inner feelings in my journal more than I openly talk about them to people.

I would recommend this book to others because if they wonder why they should bother to write in a journal, this book has a lot of suggestions about journal-writing. By writing in a journal, we as women can have a voice of our own. I finally have found that my voice is important, even if I just put that voice on paper.

Williamson, Marianne (1993) *A Woman's Worth*, New York: Random House, Inc.

This is very powerful book on women's issues written by a passionate feminist.

More Books with Good Ideas

Deep,Sam & Lyle Sussman (1996) *Yes You Can! 1200 Inspiring Ideas for Work, Home and Happiness*, Massachusetts, Addison-Wesley Publishing Company

(reviewed by Sharron) This book helped me to learn that I have the right to be me. I have the right to look after me, whether it be rest, personal care or exercise through walking or swimming. I shall not feel guilty. I have a right to do whatever makes me feel good about myself. I liked one exercise in the book where you have to write down "Yes, you can!" every time you say "I can't".

Life is a roller coaster with its ups and downs. Having this book around every day where we could pick it up and read just one line from it, would make a positive change, which I would recommend to anyone.

Eyre, Richard (1995) *Don't Just Do Something, Sit There*, New York: Simon & Shuster Inc.

Eyre takes some old cliches and rethinks them in a delightful quick read. He says, "Nothing is as good as a real rest" as opposed to "A change is as good as a rest" and "Believe in miracles" as opposed to "All you can do is all you can do". These are great discussion starters.

Green, Bob & D.G. Fulford (1993) *To Our Children's Children: Preserving Family Histories for Generations to Come*, New York: Doubleday

The stories of our families, the individuals and the events, are precious. These stories shape who we are and how we think. Greene and Fulford have developed a series of probing questions that will help you and your family members remember and document important details about the home you grew up in, your first romance and your personal dislikes. It offers great ideas for writing and exploring personal and family history.

Kremer, John (1996) *Celebrate Today!*, California: Prima Publishing

Did you know that April 3 is American Circus Day, Don't Go to Work Unless it's Fun Day, Rip Van Winkle's birthday, and the day the hat-making machine was patented? Me neither! Kremer's book is full of tidbits of information that provide reasons to celebrate even the dreariest of days.

McFarlane, Evelyn & James Saywell (1995) *If... (Questions for the Game of Life)*, New York: Random House, Inc.

There are lots of clever questions to inspire discussion or a quick writing exercise. Example: "If you could have chosen your own first name, what would it be?"

Peale, Norman Vincent (1993) *Positive Thinking Everyday*, New York: Simon & Schuster

This is a "thought a day" book, with each day providing an inspirational thought. April 25 says..."drop the three L's – lack, loss and limitation – from your vocabulary." These little sayings can often be good writing topics. We also kept a couple of "thought a day" calendars in the classroom for discussion and inspiration. Our favourite was Louise Hay's calendar called "Yes, You Can!"

Rosenbluth, Vera (1990) *Keeping Family Stories Alive*, Vancouver: Hartley & Marks

(reviewed by Alice) This book talks about memories we have and how we interpret them. Memory as a steel trap or a sieve. My mind seems to be focussed right now on a lot of painful memories, where I've been hurt. My children have also been affected, but that steel trap of my mind is slowly letting out a few good memories which I seem to have lost or covered up with bad things.

This book talks about videotaping interviews of people. We could interview people in our families and then write about some of their experiences in life – the good ones and some of the less happy times, too. Hardships and accomplishments. There are a lot of funny and fantastic stories in people's minds. It would be good to share a good story with others in the group.

St. James, Elaine (1996) *Living The Simple Life: A Guide to Scaling Down and Enjoying More*, New York: Hyperion

I found this simply written book really useful in helping the students in the Chapters Program understand "that trying to have it all has gotten in the way of enjoying the things that truly do add to our happiness and well-being". As St. James says, life "is about deciding what's important to us, and gracefully letting go of the things that aren't". This is a hard concept for people who have been so "without" all their lives. *Living the Simple Life* is full of down-to-earth suggestions for making our inner and outer lives easier, and happier.

Seaglove, Irene and Paul Bob Vehich (1996) *List Your Self – Listmaking as the Way to Self-Discovery*, Kansas City: Andrews and McMeel

(reviewed by Alice) I like the idea of making lists about thoughts and ideas instead of things you need to buy at the store. Like making a list of all the fears you have. Listing bad things and happy things helps you deal with your inner self. When you put things on paper you learn about yourself. But my first impression was that if I listed everything the book suggests, I wouldn't want other people to read it!

I really recommend this book, especially for students. Some of the lists would be fun to do together with a group. We would learn a lot about each other and about the teacher too. That would be easier for some students.

Stock, Gregory (1985) *The Book of Questions*, New York: Workman Publishing Company

___________ (1988) *The Kid's Book of Questions*, New York: Workman Publishing Company

I keep both these little Gregory Stock books in the glove compartment of my car. They're great "time passers" for long trips, and the questions make good writing topics, too. Here's a sample: #53 How do you react when people sing "Happy Birthday" to you in a restaurant?

Acknowledgements

The Research Team

Terry McGuire – My deepest thanks. Neither the Chapters Program nor this handbook would have happened or been a success without you.
Allen VandenBerg – Thanks for listening to my off the wall ideas and doing the thankless job of writing all the project reports.
Glenda Staples – Thanks for sharing your enthusiasm and expertise about Life Skills with all of us.

The Advisory Committee

Trevor Esau – New blood and new ideas are always needed. Thanks.
Pat Fahy – Another project together. How incredibly lucky I am.
Janet MacMillan – You win the prize for always being the first to respond to my faxes, letters and calls for help!
Janice Thiessen – What would I do without your clear perspective and wonderful friendship? Thanks, Jan.

The Field Testers

Thanks to you all for working through these ideas and exercises with me.

Pat Anderson at the Big Valley Educational Consortium in Drumheller
Jacqui Gillespie at Fifth on Fifth Youth Services in Lethbridge
Janet MacMillan at the Camrose Adult Read & Write Program
George Meatheringham at AVC Slave Lake in Calling Lake
Judy Murphy at the John Howard Society in Edmonton
Veronica Park at the Wetaskiwin Community Literacy Program
Marg Reine at Prospects in Edmonton
Laurie Sim at Medicine Hat College in Brooks
Glenda Staples at Medicine Hat College in Medicine Hat

and a **special thank you** to **Yvette Souque** and **Keith Anderson**, who continue to believe that I know what I'm doing.

About the Author

Over the past 16 years, Deborah Morgan has worked in the field of adult literacy as a program coordinator, tutor, instructor, researcher, writer, program developer, and special project manager. She is the Past President of the Alberta Association for Adult Literacy as well as Past President of the Literacy Coordinators of Alberta. Her first book, *Opening Doors*, documented the lived experiences of literacy workers in Alberta, Canada.

Deborah received the Canada Post 2000 Educator's Award in recognition of her groundbreaking work with the nationally acclaimed *Write to Learn Program*. She has also been honoured with the International Reading Association Carl Brawn Literacy Award in 1996, the Alberta Literacy Award of Merit in 1998 and the Camrose Chamber of Commerce Education Award in 1999.

Deborah lives in Camrose, Alberta with her family. She welcomes your comments and questions: deborah_morgan@aaal.ab.ca.

Check out the Writing Out Loud website at `writingoutloud.ca`